T0244119

SEEDS

of

HOPE

SEEDS

of

HOPE

MY JOURNEY OF SELF-DISCOVERY IN THE MEDICAL CANNABIS BUSINESS

OLUDARE ODUMOSU, MPH, PhD
CEO, Zelira Therapeutics
with Patrick O'Donnell

Skyhorse Publishing

Skyhorse Publishing books may be purchased in bulk at special discounts for sales promotion, corporate gifts, fund-raising, or educational purposes. Special editions can also be created to specifications. For details, contact the Special Sales Department, Skyhorse Publishing, 307 West 36th Street, 11th Floor, New York, NY 10018 or info@skyhorsepublishing.com.

Skyhorse® and Skyhorse Publishing® are registered trademarks of Skyhorse Publishing, Inc.®, a Delaware corporation.

Visit our website at www.skyhorsepublishing.com.

10 9 8 7 6 5 4 3 2 1

Library of Congress Cataloging-in-Publication Data is available on file.

Cover design by David Ter-Avanesyan
Cover photo: Shutterstock

ISBN: 978-1-5107-7818-4
Ebook ISBN: 978-1-5107-7900-6

Printed in the United States of America

Dedication

In loving memory of my dearest father.

This heartfelt dedication is tenderly bestowed upon the memory of my father, who departed just days after Patrick and I completed the initial draft. Though he couldn't witness the final transformation, his unwavering presence breathed life into every page. More than a father, he was my cherished companion, confidant, and guiding light.

Through trials and triumphs, his belief propelled me, shaping who I am today. He persuaded me to share this profound story, so that others may embrace the healing of the medical cannabis revolution. Dad, I am forever grateful. Your enduring spirit shall forever reside within the depths of my heart.

Contents

Introduction
On Privilege

When I began this book project back in the summer of 2018, the world was a very different place.

Thirty-five states had already established medical cannabis programs, and there was talk of legalizing cannabis on a federal level. To our north, Canada had become the first G20 country to legalize recreational use, and to our south, Mexico's Supreme Court declared that laws prohibiting responsible adult use were unconstitutional.

We had just opened our first dispensary in Plymouth Meeting. The city of Philadelphia was still buzzing from the Eagles' 41–33 Super Bowl win over the Patriots, and we had no idea that in another five years we'd be in the Big Game again, only to face a very painful loss to the Kansas City Chiefs.

Greta Thunberg hadn't yet won a Nobel Peace Prize, but she had started skipping school to protest emissions limits—raising awareness of climate change and inspiring students all over the world to follow suit.

George Floyd and Breonna Taylor were still alive. Their 2020 murders hadn't yet sparked global protests over racism and police brutality.

A US president had never lied about the dangers of a global pandemic that would claim 400,000 lives in his term alone, while also leaving millions unemployed, crippling the economy, and shutting down the country for almost two years.

We had not yet come to know of Sha'Carri Richardson or her potential . . . and the track star had not yet missed the Olympics because of a monthlong, cannabis-related suspension from the sport.

I had just turned thirty-four, and was living a dream life in south Philly. I'd been working for about a year in a high-level role at Ilera Healthcare, a medical cannabis start-up, and though the days were long and challenging, I was thrilled about my foray into this brave new frontier. The world felt like my oyster, and I felt grateful for that privilege.

Then, on the morning of October 22, my phone started buzzing earlier than usual. I grabbed it from the nightstand, blinking myself awake to what otherwise would have been a beautiful, ordinary fall morning in the city.

As Ilera's founding COO, I was used to getting urgent, early morning phone calls. But this, somehow, felt different even before I picked up. And when the voice on the other end started talking, I soon realized I wouldn't get the *privilege* to enjoy the weather, or much of anything else that

Monday: Our Google Information page had been hacked; our contact information replaced. Patients seeking our help, our guidance, would instead be unknowingly risking their medical cannabis cards by calling a black-market drug dealer who had pirated our Google page.

It was a full-blown, all-hands-on-deck emergency that, despite our best efforts, would soon blossom into a near catastrophe for our small, determined start-up.

We scrambled to fix the problem and form a response. One of our staff volunteered to alert our Facebook community to the fraudulent information. In doing so, he made two posts. The first was a screenshot showing the fraudulent information that had replaced ours on Google, and a warning that stated: "Don't jeopardize your right to use medical marijuana. Medical marijuana can only be sold through approved dispensaries with a valid medical card."

The second post, though, is where things started to unravel. Our well-meaning employee used an image of a police badge with the text, "medical marijuana is a privilege not a right."

Privilege.

One word that conveys *so much*—and, in this case, conveyed the wrong message entirely. Because access to safe, affordable cannabis-based medicine is a *right*—not a *privilege*.

And I believe the employee who made those posts, in his heart of hearts, knows that. He believes that, deep in his heart.

I believe he's eternally grateful for the work that was done by so many advocates; that has been done on the backs of so many people who suffered to bring a medical cannabis program to the state of Pennsylvania. He's one of the most gentle, selfless, committed people I've ever had the *privilege* to work with—and I still think that today.

But he was horrified, outraged, to see a bad element try to take advantage of that work. And it was an unfortunate mistake that, in the heat of that horror, that outrage, he misused one word. It was also unfortunate that back then, our team was so small we didn't have the right in-house marketing processes to vet the post and catch that simple mistake, that one word:

Privilege.

That word changed, twisted, and corrupted the message he was trying to communicate—much like that drug dealer corrupted *our* information. Because *privilege*, according to the Cambridge Dictionary, means "an advantage that only one person or group of people has, usually because of their position or because they are rich."

And what was heard; what was inadvertently screamed out to people, was that we advocated the use of law enforcement to perpetuate the war on drugs. That we advocated the use of medical cannabis only by *privileged* people.

So let me state something again, categorically: Every patient has the *right* to access their medicine. They have the *right* to live in health and wellness. Medical cannabis is a *right*—not a *privilege*—that many people have fought for; that many people have *died* for.

And as far as *privilege* is concerned, I want to state something else categorically: I was given the *privilege* to be able to humbly contribute, albeit in a small way, to the medical cannabis program through Ilera's work to win one of the five vertically integrated cannabis cultivator, processor, and dispensary operator licenses in Pennsylvania.

Only a few years ago, I never could have imagined that I'd be at the helm of a pioneering medical cannabis industry in Pennsylvania. But life takes you to unexpected places—and as we gain new insights and knowledge, the assumptions, attitudes, and opinions we've formed along the way are subject to change.

And one of the words that kept coming up during the first year of this life-changing and paradigm-shifting experience—and again when I began this book—was *privilege*. I feel like I have been blessed with many privileges throughout my life—including my journey with my family, my upbringing, education; the cutting-edge research I've done in biochemistry; the work I've done in pharmaceutical business development, and especially in my work as a founding operator of the medical cannabis program.

In the time since those early days with Ilera Healthcare, I had the *privilege* to help take the company through a very successful, multimillion-dollar sale to TerrAscend. Shortly thereafter, I was privileged to be onboarded as the first US CEO of a new Australian biopharmaceutical company called Zelira Therapeutics. In 2021, I was asked by the board to simultaneously take on the role of global managing director, and I feel privileged to remain in that dual role today.

It seems odd, then, that the word "privilege" would cause so much trouble in October 2018—trouble that even included a short-lived #BoycottIlera movement back when that Facebook post hit cyberspace. But that's because *privilege* has historically—and repeatedly—been used to deny the *rights* of others. And without careful navigation, the waters where the two intersect become treacherous.

In 2017, Ilera Healthcare became one of the first medical cannabis grower-processors licensed to operate in Pennsylvania under the state's new Medical Marijuana Program. I was privileged to be an integral part of its journey; a privilege that also cleared a path for me to achieve some of my greatest dreams: doing science and bringing good medicines and products to life. The experience has positioned me to stand at the cusp of a new frontier in pharmacology and medical care.

This book is an attempt to chronicle part of that journey—both in my own life and in the process of building a new medical cannabis program—as well as tell some of the stories I've shared only (to this point) with people very close to me. In fact, if this book had an alternate title, it would be "My Cannabis Experience: Stories I've Shared Only with Friends."

What's interesting to me, though, is that as I started to tell those stories, my friends and family helped define my understanding of my experiences. They helped me to frame my words . . . and those stories went from just living in my head to becoming the chapters of this book.

Although my story takes the form of a business memoir and traces my journey to understanding the promise and value of cannabinoid-based medicines, I found I couldn't write about that part of my experience without also including my contemplations of and engagement with the cannabis climate in which we live. So *Seeds of Hope* explores the experiences I've had as the founding COO of a medical cannabis start-up in the very strange and restrictive US climate, but also explores some of my thoughts into the history, philosophies and social constructs that have wrongly driven our cannabis journey, both as a country and as a global community.

And I want to specifically point this work toward the non-White, minority communities in the United States; people who look like me; people who have been directly affected by the war on drugs. This conversation would have been very difficult to have a few years ago; in fact for me, it would likely not have even happened just a decade ago.

But today, because I was privileged to have a series of experiences that flipped my thinking 180 degrees on a host of perspectives around my understanding of cannabis and the issues surrounding it, I feel it is my responsibility to put my thoughts and findings on paper. I hope that in doing so, I inspire more people to explore their personal understanding of cannabis. And I also hope that new understanding inspires them to challenge their thinking and perspectives where necessary; seek clarity around the issues; and participate in the push for research, scheduling reforms, and political reconsiderations not just around cannabis, but other therapeutic agents and natural compounds as well. We have opened the door onto a new world of therapies and medicines that hold great promise for the future of medicine and mankind alike. Now we must ensure it stays open, so that everyone may walk through and explore.

And as I stand at this doorway, I feel very *privileged* (and very grateful) to be a part of it all.

CHAPTER 1

"Remember the Child of Whom You Are"

"Igbo."

It's a slang term for cannabis that I heard frequently while growing up in the city of Jos, Nigeria.

Loosely translated, igbo[1] means weed, and in Nigeria it's used to refer to everything associated with the cannabis plant—from the hemp fiber extracted to make fabrics and rope to the cannabis buds selected for both medicine and recreation.

It was here in Jos, a city of about 900,000, that I first saw cannabis. I was sixteen at the time, but unlike most kids my age, I did not even know what I was looking at.

You might think that's pretty naive, but you need to understand that I was raised in a strict Baptist family, and

---

1   When capitalized, Igbo is the name for a wonderful ethnic group from the eastern region of Nigeria and has nothing to do with the slang term for cannabis.

I (mostly) toed the line. Although I could be an obnoxious kid, my parents did their best to steer me clear of trouble and bad influences—and I did my best not to disappoint them.

You see, in my culture, Yoruba—one of the largest ethnic groups in Nigeria—the oldest child carries a lot of weight on their shoulders. I was expected to be a moral beacon for my younger siblings and to provide them with an example of true leadership.

"Remember the child of whom you are," my parents and elders would say. As a child, I thought it was simply a family saying, but I as grew older, I realized it is a cultural mantra. It essentially means, "Your name is your biggest honor. Your actions can bring honor or dishonor to your name. *Don't* bring dishonor."

One of the things that could bring dishonor was being associated with cannabis. The youth of my generation grew up surrounded by antidrug messaging that all but painted the cannabis plant as evil incarnate—second only to a capital offense. Much like America, Nigeria has been gripped by its own war on drugs, and one of the most-repeated messages is the same in both countries: cannabis is a gateway drug.

As in many other countries around the world, cannabis is illegal in Nigeria. And even though a medical cannabis bill was introduced in 2020, it hasn't made much headway. The production, distribution, and use of cannabis are considered criminal offenses, and the sentences are harsh. Simple possession can land you in jail for up to four years—even for just a tiny amount. Kids under seventeen caught with cannabis face a fine and detention in a youth facility. If you sell or grow cannabis, you face life in prison.

You can imagine, then, why I took the antidrug messages to heart. The threat of being sent to a detention center—not to mention the shame it would bring to my family—were more than enough to keep me in line. Which is why, at sixteen, I had never seen cannabis in person.

And although it was more than twenty years ago, I remember the afternoon when I first laid eyes on it as if it were yesterday.

It was late 2000, and my long day of classes was coming to an end. I was enrolled in a botany program; one of the very first higher-education programs at the University of Jos. That may seem surprising, but in Nigeria it is not uncommon to complete high school and go on to college at sixteen. I'd just come out of a chemistry lab, and was getting ready to take a taxi home when I ran into some friends. In the course of exchanging stories and laughing and making some cheap shots at passersby, one of my buddies brandished a bag full of something that looked greenish-brown. "Check this out!" he said, grinning proudly. "I'm on my way to deliver it; my 'friend' has really been bugging me for his stuff."

"What is it?" I asked. "Tea leaves? Ground tobacco?"

It was as if the world had stopped spinning. You could have heard a pin drop, and it felt like everyone was staring at me. I can still see my igbo-delivering friend standing there, holding the baggie. His outfit—brown khakis, a red top, and bright, white sneakers—is branded into my memory. He looked at me incredulously and said, "You don't know what this is, pikin?[2]

Then my other friends started to laugh. I looked around, trying to figure out what the joke was.

"Oh, c'mon, 'Dare," he said. "It's good igbo, man. Gbana. Ganja. Mary Jane. Pot. Reefer. Grass. You know—weed!"

My friends passed the baggie around, sniffing its contents to assess the weed's quality. I was a little uncomfortable (*Remember the child of whom you are* ran through my mind), but more than anything, I was intrigued. There it was, this substance we'd all been warned about for so long; this mind-numbing, insanity-inducing drug—and finally seeing it in person, quite honestly, felt anticlimactic.

I suppose I had expected something very different— an awful-smelling substance, perhaps; or something that looked exotic and bizarre. But this? This was just the dried-up parts of a plant. It certainly didn't look appealing—or dangerous.

I shrugged it off, curiosity satisfied for the moment, and we all laughed as I became the new target for the

---

2   "Pikin" is a pidgin term (Nigerian slang) for "child."

cheap shots. It was getting late, so I went home, and I didn't think about that afternoon again for a long, long time.

Like I said, anticlimactic.

Little did I know that almost two decades later the controversial plant in that small baggie would play such an enormous role in my life.

For perspective, 2000 was a very bad year in parts of Nigeria. Religious riots and warfare gripped multiple regions of the country. The political and educational systems were rapidly deteriorating; there were strikes, violence and unrest that closed schools for months at a time. Schools strained under the burden of long strikes, and the education system was a mess. Before UNIJOS, I'd attended the Baptist High School in Jos, a secondary school that would be the equivalent of combining junior and senior high schools in America. My principal, a Baptist missionary from Alabama, had suggested I continue my education in the United States—a not-uncommon idea at that time.

Initially, I resisted his suggestion; my father had made it known very early on that he expected me to attend his alma mater, the prestigious University of Ife in Ile-Ife, Nigeria. That was to be my next step; leaving the shores of Nigeria was initially not even up for discussion. But the domestic strife made the idea of sending me somewhere more stable much more appealing to my parents.

My parents respected the principal and listened to his ideas carefully. He told them I had a bright future ahead of me, and that we risked wasting it if we waited for things to improve. He downplayed their worries about the expense, pointing out that it wouldn't be as bad as they feared, and that scholarships could help. "Let him take the requisite exams and see how he does first. Then you can figure out the rest," he said.

I'd had a number of friends and acquaintances who'd gone on to various American universities, but there were a lot of familiar faces at Calvin College (now Calvin University), in Grand Rapids, Michigan. That helped bump it to the top of our list. And so in 2001 my life took a 180-degree turn from its expected course, and I found myself leaving my home country for the first time, on my way to the Great Lakes State and the land of opportunity.

Calvin and America were big transitions for me—don't forget I was just seventeen—but my friends and the university community helped me to settle into my new life pretty quickly. Four years seemed to just fly by. "Remember the child of whom you are" was my mantra not so much by choice, but because I'd heard it every single day of my life. It ran like an undercurrent in my mind, framing every decision I made. I worked hard, and I was a model international student.

After receiving my bachelor's degree in 2005, I went on to Loma Linda University School of Public Health in California, where I earned a master's degree in public health epidemiology in 2007. I immediately started working toward a PhD in biochemistry from the Loma Linda

University School of Medicine. Life as a grad student in California was engaging, fast-paced, and very fulfilling. I would often stop and reflect on the fact that my choices were making my parents proud ("Remember the child of whom you are"), and I felt a sense of satisfaction and honor.

My research caught the eye of the scientific community, and my scientific accomplishments led to offers from notable institutions and life science industry leaders. At graduation in 2011, I was the sole recipient of the dean's award for the School of Medicine's Basic Science program—a very proud moment for my parents.

Shortly after graduation, I accepted a position as a business development manager for Iroko Pharmaceuticals, a start-up pharmaceutical company in Philadelphia focused on bringing novel therapeutic improvements through the development of effective low-dose nonsteroidal anti-inflammatory drugs (NSAIDs). By 2013, I was promoted to senior business development manager.

It seemed like I'd done it: I'd worked hard and earned my place in the world.

As a stamp of independence, I got a tattoo—something forbidden by my father as long as I was under his roof or financial umbrella. But now I was a young, upcoming success story, working my way up the corporate ladder. I had a high-rise apartment on the Parkway in downtown Philly. I'd made my parents proud and was well on my way to bringing honor to the family name. The only way for me to go now was up.

But by 2016, all that would change, in ways the younger me could never have imagined. I faced a decision that involved a great deal of risk—to my future, to my finances, and—at least in the eyes of my parents—to my family's honor.

And while I weighed the pros and cons of that decision, one phrase still kept running through my mind:

"Remember the child of whom you are."

CHAPTER 2

"I Am Alive"

Bear with me as I backtrack a bit.

I didn't try cannabis until I was twenty-six. By today's standards, that's pretty remarkable for a kid from Nigeria—pretty remarkable almost anywhere you're from, really. In my home country, despite severe legal penalties, cannabis has been part of the unspoken culture among the youth and upwardly mobile working class for a long time. Still, I very carefully steered clear of it—and with good reason: "Remember the child of whom you are."

I grew up in the city of Jos, where as I mentioned earlier, I went to Baptist High School. Back then it was one of the top boarding schools in the city, and—with the weight of the family name on my shoulders—I was expected to set a very high bar for my brothers. I didn't disappoint . . . at first.

I was a prefect, a senior student leader with the authority to enforce school rules and regulations. I studied hard and was always at or near the top of my class. I ran track. And I (almost) always followed "the rules." Like any kid, though, I wanted to be liked.

Some of my friends at the time were, shall we say, a little *less* mindful of those rules than I (one of those friends being the guy from chapter 1 who was delivering weed!).

And so, one evening when we were returning from a track meet at another school, I decided to walk back with my friends instead of taking the school bus.

There, on the fringes of a busy car park, the air was thick with noise, anticipation, and the excitement that comes with freedom, however brief. And while the smells of frying food wafted around us and the shouts of bus drivers announcing destinations hung in the air, I broke down and succumbed to peer pressure for the first time.

Did I drink a beer? Try drugs? Make plans to skip a class?

No. I took a puff of a friend's cigarette.

That's right. Just a cigarette. It didn't seem like a big deal at the time. But weeks later, my friends and I were called into a conference room. I knew trouble was coming.

It turns out someone—one of those friends, in fact— had reported us. Called in for some other infraction, he sang like a canary in the hopes of a little leniency. He even spilled the beans about our walk back from the game, and that shared cigarette.

Smoking anything, of course—tobacco included— was against school policy, but to make matters worse, some of those friends had a "rap sheet." Now, even though I'd had just *one single puff* of a cigarette, I was being lumped in with them, and was being punished for other things I'd never done.

For that single puff, that momentary lapse in judgment, I paid a heavy price: I was flogged, suspended for two weeks, lost my prefect badge and all the privileges that went with it, and—perhaps worst of all—I had to tell my parents the news.

I was mortified at the prospect, and my heart was heavy with shame at the knowledge I'd let them down. The saving grace, however, was that my parents had a policy with us: No matter how bad it is, we want to hear it from you. We'll believe you over someone else.

And so my parents turned it into a teachable moment, and instead of feeling shame, I learned from my mistake. One of the lessons came from a book they gave me: *John Ploughman's Talk*, by Charles Spurgeon. "Go with your neighbor as far as good conscience will go with you," Spurgeon wrote, "but part company where the shoe of conscience begins to pinch your foot."

As you can see, the rules at my school were positively draconian. The severe punishments never fit the crime. Our Nigerian laws, cultural expectations, and mores differ as well. If you're convicted of cannabis possession, the *minimum* jail sentence is twelve years. And just smoking *tobacco* is considered shameful—if you had any adult relatives who smoked, they would take great pains to hide it from the family.

And so that single incident with a cigarette informed my view of peer pressure, and I vowed never again to allow myself to get into that position, with tobacco or anything else.

Then there was the propaganda for Nigeria's war on drugs, which was ubiquitous when I was growing up. Kids heard about the evils of cannabis from every corner. We were taught that simply trying a joint could drive someone crazy; that a few puffs of a blunt would lead you to a short, unhappy life filled with needles or white powder or both.

At church, our preacher said things like, "Marijuana will numb your mind. It's the devil's creation!" During a discussion at a family gathering, a well-meaning aunt told me, "Those who use igbo end up in mental institutions." In school, a teacher told us, "A joint has more carcinogens than cigarettes."

The antidrug message even informed the psychology of our playtime. Much like the United States had Nancy Reagan's "this is your brain on drugs" frying-egg commercial on repeat during afternoon cartoons, there was a push in Nigeria, at every level, to dissuade children from the evils of mind-altering substances.

One of the more insidious attacks that I remember was delivered through popular music. A song called "Omode," by Nigerian artist Funmi Adams, was about making good choices—like listening to your parents, being respectful, being content with what you have rather than being envious of others. And of course, there was an antidrug stanza, too. The message was pretty straightforward: cannabis will ruin your life.

"Omode" was getting a lot of airplay at the time, and whenever it came on, my brothers and I would do our best to belt out the lyrics. Roughly translated to English, they were:

"Children, wherever you are,
open up your ears and hear me,
marijuana may look like fun, but drugs will kill you.
You see homeless madmen on the street . . ."

And so on, and so on, and so on.

With this culture of disinformation surrounding me, it's no wonder that the older I got, the more convinced I became that cannabis was evil. Looking back, I think it's kind of interesting that I was so brainwashed because I was a naturally curious kid.

But somehow, I ignored all the peer pressure, and even ignored the facts (there were some, even back then) that ran counter to the prevailing message: "Marijuana is a gateway drug. Marijuana will ruin your life. Marijuana is evil." I just took in the propaganda and accepted what I was told, without question.

And so, naivete firmly engrained, I was surprised when I first arrived at Calvin that there were plenty of opportunities to try cannabis if I wanted to—just like there would have been at any other school.

But "remember the child of whom you are" and the antidrug messaging were rooted deep within me, so I just said "No," like Nancy Reagan advised, and kept my nose in my books until I graduated. I took the same philosophy with me when I headed to Loma Linda.

As you probably know, cannabis is generally accepted in California. It's a part of beach life; it's a part of mountain life—it's everywhere, and has been for a long time. (It was approved for medical use in 1996, and responsible adult use in 2016.) While studying at Loma Linda, I was spending a lot of time in Big Bear, Palm Desert, Huntington Beach, San Diego, and Idyllwild—and once again, I was surrounded by opportunities to try cannabis.

But I *still* refused.

In fact, it was so deeply ingrained in me that cannabis was mind-numbing, that it was a gateway drug, that I advocated *against* it.

My beliefs—which were so strong they could have passed for dogma—led to a lot of heated conversations and even some full-on arguments about cannabis with my friends and a girl I was dating. They all tried to persuade me to "just try it," but still I would say things like "No way. . . . I'm working on my doctorate, why would I want to numb my mind?" I was very adamant: Cannabis had *no place* in my life. You'd have been hard-pressed to find someone who was more against its use than me.

That all changed in 2011, when I was hands-, feet-, and neck-deep into preparations for my dissertation defense.

I was doing everything in my power to stay focused on my thesis, but before I knew it, I was overwhelmed.

I wasn't sleeping. I could not concentrate. And everything came to a head one week when I had been awake for well over seventy-two hours. I'd heard people say that not sleeping for twenty-four hours is a lot like being drunk, so can you imagine the tricks my mind was playing on me at this point? Can you imagine my emotional state?

Science tells us that when extreme sleep deprivation occurs, you go into what's called "microsleep"—it's like short naps where you zone out, but you don't realize your brain is going into a dream state, and you feel like you're hallucinating.

For me, it also felt like I was dying. My body was falling apart, and I'd feel like I wasn't even *in* my own body. I would go to my lab and somehow muddle through my experiments, then go lie down on my favorite couch, but my anxious mind was racing along with my pulse, and I wasn't able to fall asleep. Even I could tell that my pace, my mojo, was gone. I was really struggling.

I was lucky to have really good friends around me at that time. They would try to cheer me up and keep me focused. I will be forever indebted to those guys, but I still couldn't sleep!

One of those friends stopped by and, seeing my condition, offered me a legally available, brand-name sleep aid. At that point, I was ready to try anything—and back then, a prescription drug was something that felt safe to me. After all, it was a legal, frontline therapy for sleep disorders. What could possibly go wrong?

Imagine this, then: I'm going on day four or five with no sleep. I take the pill, and wait for sleep to come. I wait and wait for sleep through the night, but still find myself wide awake—and now with an even worse feeling of tiredness. At one point, I remember thinking to myself, "If I don't sleep tonight I think I will die." And I *truly* believed it.

At that point, a dear friend of mine—let's call him Joe (not his real name)—said sarcastically, "You should try weed. It'll help you sleep."

I briefly considered his offer, but still wouldn't relent. It would be illegal, I reasoned.

And then another friend—let's call him Jack (not his real name)—echoed my fears, saying: "You'd better do something about sleeping tonight—*you look like you're going to die.*"

True or not, it didn't take much persuasion beyond that. My mind was a sleep-deprived jumble of confusion and emotion. I'd resisted peer pressure for so long, but now I was more afraid of death than of trying this plant that I'd been avoiding like the plague.

Still, I decided I was going to go through the proper channels. "Can you get me to a doctor who can write a prescription?" I asked (I didn't even know the right terminology then). "If I'm going to try it, I want to do it legally."

So, my ever-patient friends took me to a doctor, who wrote me a recommendation. I then walked into a dispensary, but of course didn't have a *clue* about what I was ordering or even looking at. I vaguely remember realizing I was in a clean, well-organized room that had a remarkable, distinct smell and was filled with packaged cannabis. Thankfully, the associate—who I now know is called a "budtender"—could tell it was my first time.

"What condition are you trying to treat?" he asked. I told him I couldn't sleep.

"Then you need a kush, man," he said immediately. It's generally believed that strains associated with kush are useful for helping with sleep. The budtender was kind, taking his time to walk me through a number of different strains and providing information I most certainly did not have at the time. My head was spinning. This wasn't what I'd been taught!

I got home later that evening, and with the help of Joe—who made a ceremony out of rolling my very first joint—I took a few puffs.

This was my first time trying cannabis, and I had no idea what to expect. I waited for it to kick in. I waited, and I waited, and waited, and waited. I remember opening my eyes at some point and it felt like only five minutes had passed, but no, it wasn't five minutes later. It was 7 o'clock the next morning! I had slept for about *nine hours*!

I woke up very naturally. I woke up feeling renewed. My head was clear; the cobwebs had melted away. It was almost unbelievable. I briefly thought something bad had happened—had I hallucinated it all? Maybe I'd been asleep for only five minutes, and this was just my imagination. But as I think back on it today, of all the things I've ever desired in life, having a sleep as deep, as refreshing, as natural as that one was, is at the top of my list.

As a scientist, I was immediately processing all that I was feeling in my body. I could tell that I'd had a physiological response; a complete restoration from the state I'd been in for days. I remember thinking, "This does not make sense. Someone needs to help me unlearn everything I have been taught. Have I been lied to all my life? Am I the exception to the rule? Because this so-called evil plant has just done the exact opposite of what I was told it would do. It has actually helped me, not made me insane or stupid. Someone needs to talk—I have time, I'll wait!"

For the first time, I was seeing this plant in a whole new light. I wasn't sure if I needed to forgive myself for being misled, or find a way to forgive those who'd fed me so much bullshit for so many years.

To have an experience like that, the first time I tried cannabis . . . It's an understatement to say it was a lot to process. And suddenly, a flood of emotion just came rushing over me. I couldn't separate whether it was from the joy of being able to sleep, or relief because I didn't die, or a feeling that maybe I should have done this a long time ago . . . or even the guilt I felt, because I was thinking, "This very same thing that I thought was illegal, that was going to numb my mind, that was so *terrible* for me and everyone else . . . was what ultimately allowed me to get a good night of sleep."

I continued to use cannabis as needed to help with my sleep, and it worked every time. Mind-numbing? Hardly! I would wake up in the morning with a clear mind, and that felt really good. I felt like I had my mojo back. And *wow*! My perception of this plant, this product, had completely changed. I had gone from "This thing will kill you" to "This plant saved me. Because of this plant, I am alive."

Because I really, honestly had thought I was going to die that night from lack of sleep. My world, my mind, my body was a wreck.

Who knows what really would have happened? All I know is that one recommendation, that single, legal first step, changed my life, forever, for the better. I was able to start unpacking a lifetime of disinformation simply because I was in the right place at the right time. The state of California had been one of the first states to recognize that access to cannabis is a right, and because of that, I was privileged to be able to learn the truth firsthand.

It was *literally* my eureka moment—and one for which I will always be thankful.

CHAPTER 3

"My Son Has Lost His Mind!"

By mid-2016, I felt like I was on top of the world.

As I mentioned in chapter 1, I was now working as senior business development manager for Iroko Pharmaceuticals. My role could be described as that of a "translational scientist"—I supported the development and validation of Iroko's products through clinical trials and regulatory approvals by the Federal Drug Administration through to market entry.

My career was blossoming, and I felt things were going exactly as they should. The stressors of college and my dissertation long behind me, I no longer needed medical cannabis to help me sleep—and thank goodness, since that right had not yet been recognized in Pennsylvania.

I had just completed an unconventional long-term assignment in which I'd been "loaned" to our sales department in New York City. To say the project had exceeded expectations is an understatement. I had returned to

Philadelphia feeling like a veritable rock star. The Eagles might not yet have won a Super Bowl, but I certainly felt like I had. Maybe I was channeling some energy they would pick up on in 2018.

Let me explain—but for that, I have to take us even further back, to 2014.

I like to learn, and as part of that, I set challenges for myself around my birthdays. For my thirtieth, I decided to create a custom eyewear business. I was inspired after ordering a pair of glasses online and wondering if the plastic frames could be made from more sustainable materials at a lower cost. I did my research, and found there was a growing demand for my idea. I also found there were a number of eyewear companies already using sustainable materials, but their products were quite expensive. I started by finding design partners who shared my vision, and we worked together to create a line of affordable eyewear that was both stylish and sustainable. Once we had the designs and the materials in place, I put together a business plan. I then borrowed Osagie's office to launch "Yoeyes" on my birthday. It was successful right from the start, and I ran Yoeyes on the side for the next few years before winding it up to focus solely on my role at Ilera.

Around the same time that I launched Yoeyes, Iroko launched its first FDA-approved low-dose NSAIDs, and after spending almost three years in the office working on them, I was feeling restless. I was excited about other opportunities the products might hold for my growth within the company—and I knew those opportunities, which were on the commercial side, lay beyond the four walls of our brick-and-mortar building. I went to my boss and said, "Give me a new challenge, something exciting."

I envisioned being transitioned into corporate development, or perhaps even sent to work on the licensing process for something new. In comparison, the response I received came out of left field.

Because I knew the product inside and out, the management team had decided it would be a *great* idea if I was sent to New York to take on an entire sales territory by myself—which meant I would be a product rep, carrying a bag in the streets, pitching to doctors, and closing sales.

And all I could think was, *Wait . . . sales?*

Yes. Sales.

Just like that, I found myself faced with an entirely new—albeit temporary—role. Exciting? Sure. But I needed time to consider it. Because I had no sales experience. Not even a little. And I wasn't exactly headed into friendly territory, either.

On one side, you had my boss and the head of sales. They thought it would be a good learning experience for me, an opportunity to cross-train. I would be sent into a region they were thinking of shutting down anyway, so if nothing came out of it, there'd be no loss. And if the experiment was successful, it would be a win.

On the other side, you had the regional sales manager I would report to, and a massive sales team that Iroko had just hired. The manager's knee-jerk reaction was, "Why are you sending me some guy with zero experience? He's just going to be a nuisance. This makes no sense."

He was so outraged over being sent such a complete novice, in fact, that he wrote the powers that be a letter, the essence of which was "Are you people *nuts*? What the hell is wrong with you?"

The sales team was equally skeptical. They probably wondered if I was a spy or if I was there to sabotage them. I knew I'd have to tread carefully and prove myself a team player. It would not be an easy assignment.

But once I realized the opportunity being placed in front of me, it was like the song from *Hamilton*: I was *not* throwing away my shot. So I sucked it up and put my shoulder down and plowed forward. And I did it happily, too. No matter how they felt in New York, I didn't let it faze me.

Still, there was a part of me that spent a lot of time thinking, "Why do I *always* have to jump headfirst into the deep end? Is there something wrong with me?"

Fast-forward six months, however, and we're looking at an entirely different story. That same regional sales manager who thought I'd just get in the way is now asking if I can stay on even longer.

So, what happened?

Well, despite being the new guy, I'd managed to blow all their expectations out of the water.

I'd not only saved a dying business territory that was on the verge of being shut down, but I'd also helped it to grow—taking it to a top-tier sales territory. By way of numbers, in those six months I'd made the President's Circle and earned a bonus that was almost as big as my baseline salary.

I'd pushed my reservations and fear to the side, tackled a new opportunity head-on and, despite having no experience, *literally* came out on top.

I'd taken my shot, and I'd won big. To my mind, rockstar big. And so there I was, back in Philadelphia in 2016, feeling nearly untouchable.

Until the carpet was yanked right out from under my feet.

It turns out that being a so-called rock star doesn't always keep one dry when the corporate storms hit. Iroko Pharmaceuticals, where I had worked for almost five years, was downsizing. My department was being hit hard—and my job was one of those on the chopping block.

On one level, I knew this was "just business." I knew this was a corporate decision, not something aimed at me personally. But on another level, I couldn't help myself. I took it *very* personally. I was rattled. After all, hadn't I just more than proved my worth?

But now, as I look back, I can say that I think it worked out well . . . maybe even better than I could have expected. I accepted the severance package, which was very attractive—I'd even say fantastic. I left on the best of terms, grateful that I'd been privileged to work at such an innovative, forward-thinking company. And I'd been given a rare opportunity to see the industry from both sides of the lens.

Yet looking forward, I suddenly found my career path lacked a clear direction.

In those first few weeks of my unemployment, I intentionally blocked out everything and invested time in myself. I was exercising, reading, expanding my culinary skill set, socializing, and generally setting my mind in order. I was determined not to let the layoff bother me.

But it was there, knocking at the door in my mind. And the minute I opened it, all that anxiety came flooding in. My brain went into overdrive. *What are you going to do next? Are you going to stay in pharma? Are you going to do something else? Maybe you should make a few calls.*

It felt like I'd let a golden retriever into my head, and it was chasing my thoughts around and around in ever-tightening circles.

Fortunately, from a financial perspective, the severance package gave me enough money to live on for the next four to six months. At least I wouldn't have to worry about being homeless . . . at least, not for a while. And knowing my parents would be frantic, I decided to spare them the news and swore other family members to secrecy.

After about a month, I put feelers out. And despite my fears, offers started pouring in from all over. Companies in California, New York, New Jersey—even international companies were interested. Now I had my pick.

I was getting my mojo back. The world felt like my oyster again. But I soon found that I couldn't give those offers the attention they deserved because my mind was elsewhere.

All across the United States, a movement had been growing that I'd locked on to. Its potential for explosive growth—especially right here, in Pennsylvania—held my focus, and I was turning a blind eye to *all* those great opportunities. I felt like it was imperative that I stay put, even though another part of me would have relished a return to California or the adventure of moving somewhere altogether new.

In the back of my mind, I justified my waiting game by making a deal with myself: if that movement didn't reach Pennsylvania soon, I'd revisit those earlier opportunities and redouble my efforts.

But then, on April 17, 2016, Pennsylvania Gov. Tom Wolf placed his signature on Act 16—the medical cannabis bill.

And I wanted in.

Given my previous stance on cannabis, that may seem like a surprising decision. But after my experience during graduate school, I had become convinced that there were unexplored medicinal benefits to the cannabis plant. I had followed the progress of medical cannabis for a few years now and was intrigued by the evolution of information in the space.

And then, like something out of a movie script, an opportunity practically landed in my lap.

* * *

It was November 11, and I had been invited to the Philadelphia Business Hall of Fame induction for Osagie Imasogie, my mentor and the founder and CEO of Iroko, my previous employer. Also at the dinner table were Zoltan Kerekes and Lisa Gray, who, along with Osagie, would later become Ilera Healthcare's founding board members.

At some point in the evening, conversation turned to the April law that had established the Pennsylvania Medical Marijuana Program. And to my pleasant surprise, it wasn't long before the group was discussing plans to apply for one of the licenses to grow, process, and dispense medical cannabis in Pennsylvania. My eyes popped open.

It seemed a seed I'd planted might have taken root.

You see, much earlier in the year I'd had a discussion with Osagie about medical cannabis. "It might be a smart business opportunity to explore if it's legalized in Pennsylvania," I said.

Osagie has more than thirty-five years of experience in pharmaceuticals, including managing drug development based on natural compounds. So the idea of cannabis-based medicine immediately made sense to him—but he also understood the challenges presented by the legal and political climate of the day.

We were walking down the steps of the Philadelphia Auto Show at the time, and he turned to me and replied, "'Dare, of all the great ideas you mentioned today, let's just say I like the medical cannabis option, but it's going to take a lot of thought. I hear you. I'm always open to new knowledge. Let me talk to my partners and see what comes out of it."

You can see why I was thrilled when it came up at the dinner table. It meant that Osagie really had talked to his partners. And as we were talking about the application process, I was even more surprised that Zoltan's wife, Diane, was excited to tell me she had been doing some research and had found a potential option, a Yoruba name for the company: Ilera.

Pronounced "e-LAY-ra," the word means health, wellness, and healing. It was perfect—appropriate not only because of its meaning, but also because it upheld Osagie's tradition of giving meaningful Yoruba names to companies he'd founded.

During the rest of that dinner, my brain was stuck in interview mode—it was like I couldn't stop myself. I told them I could help. I told them I could do research. I told them I'd do whatever it took.

I may even have told them, "You don't have to pay me right away. I'll work at risk."

I was childishly, unabashedly interviewing right then and there for a job—any job—related to this cannabis opportunity.

* * *

Not long after, when they were putting together their application, Lisa called me. My name was being considered for head of business marketing. I don't recall even letting her finish her thoughts before I said "Yes!" Though frankly speaking, if she had told me the position of chief coffee maker in the staff cafeteria was available, I would have taken it.

I was giddy about it. I could not *wait* to get started. A few weeks later, though, when I sat down to discuss the job with Lisa, she told me, "We've changed our minds."

My heart skipped a beat, and I sucked in my breath. All the sounds in the room faded. *They changed their minds,* I thought. *This can't be good.*

The space of a few seconds seemed to stretch out into ten minutes, and I thought, "I turned down other opportunities for this! I passed up on excellent offers all in the hopes that I'd get a job in this space. And now that I'm so close . . ."

But then, like a distant voice down a well, I heard Lisa continue, "How does COO sound?"

At that moment, sitting in Lisa's office in my gray suit and a big, checkered purple shirt with no tie, you would *think* the first thing that hit me was relief and excitement.

What hit me next, though, was *COO? What are they thinking?*

And that was immediately followed by a more important thought: "Well, these are some of the brightest people

I know. They must see something in me that I have yet to see in myself. All three of them together cannot be crazy. So boy, you'd better step the f**k up."

I was ready to take my shot. Again.

Returning to earth, all I did for a few seconds was stare at Lisa. And all I managed to get out was a chuckle and "Oh my goodness, really?"

Lisa handed me my own résumé, then, and told me why they thought I'd be a good fit. They'd watched me grow at Iroko as I worked my way through corporate development, operational management, cross-continental projects, and US and global licensing . . . even daring to take on the sales role in New York. "We've also watched you build and grow a few of your own businesses success- fully on the side," she said.

"We love you for this role because you are not afraid," she continued. "This is a new space, a new program, and we need somebody who is not afraid to try new things, who has their eyes set on success. And when we looked around, we couldn't find a better person for that role than you. All the partners feel the same way. I just happen to be the one delivering the good news to you."

Of course, I was keenly aware that this job was still hypothetical. Everything would depend on winning one of the state's coveted "super" licenses to grow, process, and sell medical cannabis. If we didn't win it, come June 2017 none of this would matter anyway—and I'd be out looking for a job again.

But I had a very good feeling about our prospects, and I'd learned a lot about perseverance over the last few years. My confidence was high.

Of course, everything I'd faced up to now had been relatively easy, compared to what was coming next:

I still had my very traditional, very anti-cannabis parents back in Nigeria to convince.

* * *

It's true. Telling my parents would be the hardest part of this whole experience for me.

Remember the child of whom you are was on repeat in the back of my mind. I'd had a very personal experience with cannabis that had shown me, quite clearly, all the BS I'd been fed since childhood. My parents hadn't had the benefit of that experience—and they'd been fed cannabis misinformation a *lot* longer than I.

How was I going to show them the light?

My first step, I knew, would have to be getting the rest of my family on board. That might seem odd to you, but for me it was essential. I have always valued my family's opinion. Maybe that's just how my father wired his boys. So, I talked to my brothers, making them swear again and again they wouldn't tell our parents. "This could turn out to be the opportunity of a lifetime," I said. "It's a brand-new program; I don't know what to expect." I explained to them that the probability for success was real—but there was also a very real potential for failure.

I was willing to face that risk, I told them, because something deep inside me would not let me walk away from this. It was, at best, a wildcard, but on some level, I could not shake the feeling that this wildcard would turn out to be an ace.

I can honestly say now that the prospect of committing seven months of my life, unpaid, to the pursuit of a license had me feeling both scared out of my mind *and* strangely confident. Thankfully, the confidence won out. They could tell I was resolute. I was on a roll, and I didn't stop with my brothers.

I went on a family campaign.

I talked about it with my aunts, uncles, cousins, and friends—at least the ones I thought could keep my secret. By early December, I had reached critical mass and had the family behind me. I knew it was finally time to tell my parents.

But despite all of that buildup, I still couldn't bring myself to do it.

So, I devised a new plan. My brother was to be married in the middle of December, during the holiday season. I reasoned that everyone would be happy, and by riding the coattails of those good feelings to spring my news, I'd be able to offset the shock I was about to deliver.

Mind you, I had been out of a job for three months already—and they still didn't know.

So, I steeled myself for the big talk. I went to my brother's wedding, prepared to deliver my news. *This is it!* I told myself.

And then I thought, *If this goes badly, I am ending my parents' year on a bad note. And I'll diminish the joy of my brother's wedding, too. I can't do that.* So, fearless and considerate soul that I am, I waited until January. Waited, in fact, until the very day I was leaving to return to the United States.

Fearless, indeed.

Suitcases packed and ready to go, I walked into my parents' bedroom, where they were both sitting propped up against the headboard. I was standing near the foot of the bed, looking down at them—and it was like a scene from a sitcom.

"Mom, Dad, I don't have a job. I left Iroko in September."

My parents looked at each other, then back at me, and they were both quiet. You could have heard a pin drop.

I said, "It's okay, though. I'm fine."

"Did something happen?" Mom asked, worry creeping into her voice.

"Yes, but not something bad."

She let out a deep sigh of relief, and before she could ask any more questions, I seized the moment to begin my pitch.

I explained the severance package, and that by my calculations, my savings would ensure I was well taken

care of for at least the next nine months while I looked
for a new employer. I told them that I had plenty of good
prospects. I told them I'd left on good terms, through no
fault of my own. I thought all my explanations and reassurances would put them at ease . . . but no.

Already my mother looked like the entire world was
falling apart. She moved to the edge of the bed and swung
her feet to the ground. Dad did the same. While I talked,
they edged closer and closer until somehow, they were
both sitting right in front of me, almost before I noticed.

Tension gripped their bodies. Worry flooded their
faces. And I hadn't even *mentioned* what I was going
to do next: Join a medical cannabis group as an *unpaid*
employee. You could almost feel my mother's heart jump
out of her chest when I said, "But there is more."

They looked at me expectantly. It felt like the roof was
about to cave in.

I summoned up the last of my courage and soldiered
on. "I'm joining this group called Ilera. We're applying
for a medical cannabis license."

I saw the confusion on my mother's face as she looked
at my father, and realized she didn't grasp the implications of what I had just said. I had to speak in a language
they understood. So I used the slang term instead: igbo.

That's when all hell broke loose.

First my mother rocked back and forth there on
the foot of the bed, almost like she was trying to keep
from throwing herself straight to the floor, wailing and

shrieking. Then she clapped her hands to her head, and I knew I had to work fast. Because whenever a Nigerian mother claps her hands to her head, it does not end well.

In this particular moment, it meant: "My son has lost his mind! He's been brainwashed by the devil himself! I tried my best to raise him right; why have you forsaken me, O Lord?"

Without her having said a single word, I knew my mother thought I had *completely* lost it. Written all over her face was, "I don't know who this is in front of me. Where is my son, and what have you done with him?"

On the other side of the bed, my father's face was a mask of confusion. Then his eyes narrowed and focused on me with such a piercing look that I momentarily considered abandoning the rest of my pitch and telling them the whole thing was a big prank!

I resisted the urge, though, and held fast. I reminded them that they trusted me. I reminded them that they trusted Osagie, my previous employer . . . but to no avail. They just didn't understand, because in their view, cannabis was the stuff that was numbing people's minds, turning them into madmen, killing them.

Every one of their words was heavy with concern and confusion. "Remember the child of whom you are," they said. "You're not getting a real job. You're working for a company that is making igbo—ganja! Our son has gone crazy. Our son has lost his mind! What will the rest of the family say? What will the *world* say?"

Aha! That was the moment I'd been waiting for: What would the world say? Because it gave me the opportunity to say, "Actually, the world is okay with it. And this is why you should be, too." I ran them through the list of people who already knew, and how they'd reacted to the news.

"I even told Grandpa!" I said—and that, perhaps, was the clincher.

You could see now in their eyes a realization that maybe they didn't understand the issue as well as they'd thought; that maybe there are virtues to medical cannabis that were beyond the scope of their experience. It was as if knowing that other family members were okay with it brought them some weird comfort; that maybe, just maybe, there could be something redeemable about this whole "situation" that was momentarily beyond their grasp.

As a Yoruba boy, you learn that the sound of deep breaths from your elders can have many meanings. There are those that convey confusion; others that convey panic and fear; some that convey frustration or exasperation. The deep breaths my parents were taking that day seemed to convey, "We don't know what to say right now, but we'll leave it all in God's hands."

After that, we said a weird, strained goodbye. Yet I left feeling oddly satisfied with our conversation. As strange as this may sound, I had a feeling that I'd made some kind of a breakthrough; that even though my success wasn't evident now, it would become so later. I felt that this was the best I could get . . . that for now, I had won. I flew home knowing that they would accept my decision—at least for the time being.

But of course, that was not the end of it. We had many, *many* more conversations about my new role after that. They called me *every day* for the next month.

"We're just trying to help," my mother would say.

To their credit, over the next several months while I was "jobless" and "working at my own risk" for an "igbo" company that "might" get a license, you could see my parents struggle to find the right questions to ask me to reach across the table. I saw a new side to them—to my father especially. I saw them go from being instructors to being students.

It's a very humbling experience when you see that kind of shift in your parents. I couldn't help but be proud of them. Even though they were confused, they allowed their faith in me to lead the way as they struggled through that confusion. Eventually, I saw them join their faith with mine as we waited in expectation for the date the announcement would be made. My parents even said they'd pray for me; pray that this venture would be successful.

And I'll never forget that fateful day—June 20, 2017—when I announced that we had been awarded our license; that Ilera was moving from hope to reality. I called my mother using FaceTime, and upon hearing the good news, she broke out into a dance that was interspersed with shouts of "Hallelujah!"

My father, hearing all the commotion, came to see what was going on. When he saw his dancing wife, she beckoned to him to join her, and he did so without any hesitation—without even knowing what he was celebrating. Because in my culture, dancing is a common reaction to good news. Soon, their dancing turned to prayers for God's direction and blessings upon the new venture. I knew then that the hardest part of this journey was over.

Of course, as typical parents they then had a million questions. And when we ended our FaceTime chat, there was still a little fear in their voices. But mostly, it was overwhelming pride and relief.

I finally felt like I'd brought honor to the family name again. "Remember the child of whom you are" could once more be said with pride, not admonishment.

And I was now beginning the most exciting adventure of my life.

CHAPTER 4

Highs and Lows

Although I now had the promise of a job, it was conditional, and I was working "at risk"—meaning I wasn't getting paid for my time. And I was putting in *a lot* of time: ten- to twelve-hour days were the norm, with several fourteen- and sixteen-hour days sprinkled in for good measure.

But I understood that those long hours were all worthwhile. Everyone was highly motivated, knowing that of all the applicants that had won a license in the first round, if anyone could create pharmaceutical-grade medicines from cannabinoids, it was our team. Our leadership already had an impressive background in pharmaceutical drug development and commercialization, and we knew we had the grit and determination to do the impossible and actualize this license and operationalize it in just a few months' time. And as a result, we knew patients in the state of Pennsylvania were closer than ever to being able to legally access cannabis-based medicine. It was an exciting, albeit highly stressful, time.

To complicate matters, I knew that if the state didn't award Ilera with a license to grow and process medical cannabis, I'd be facing a new job search with most of my savings used up and no severance package. Yet I still felt privileged to be a part of this process.

I was hopeful, and determined, and glad I was taking this chance. Long before *Hamilton* was even a thing, hockey great Wayne Gretzky once said, "You miss 100 percent of the shots you don't take." I will forever remain grateful that I took this shot.

And even though I was really afraid—who wouldn't be?—I knew, on some level, that even if Ilera lost its bid, I would have forever been filled with regret if I hadn't taken the shot. Because you have to dare to give something to get something, and no matter the outcome, this was going to be a life-changing experience. It was also something I felt I had to do, because it was long past time to end the drug war and return the right to medical cannabis to the people. And in light of my own experiences, I felt like I had a personal responsibility to take up the cannabis mantle and push back on all those years of disinformation and repression.

I had decided, days before the June 2017 license announcement would come, to travel to California on my own dime to observe cannabinoid extraction. The knowledge would be useful if we won, and still useful if we didn't. Besides, I really needed to escape the chatter in Philadelphia, which was crippling. Some people felt confident they knew who would win and who wouldn't—and Ilera was not on their "winners" list, since we were not a recognized Pennsylvania bigwig!

I'd stay in California through June 21, a day after the announcement. I figured I'd get a small vacation out of the trip and, if we didn't win, I wouldn't be in the city for the "shame party."

On the night of June 18, my friend Wale called and informed me he was buying a last-minute ticket to be with me in California for the announcement. He said, "You shouldn't party by yourself if you do win, and you sure shouldn't be miserable by yourself if you don't win!"

At about 9:59 a.m. PST on June 20th, Wale knocked on my door, two coffees in hand. We stood in my hotel room, eyes glued to the clock, waiting for it to turn to 10 a.m.—which would be 1 p.m. Eastern time, when the Pennsylvania Department of Health was scheduled to announce the winners. It was only one minute, but it felt like an eternity as the seconds ticked by.

We stood, eyes and ears glued to the webcast. You can imagine my racing thoughts, my anxiety, as I painfully listened to every word that came out of the mouth of John Collins, director of the state's Office of Medical Marijuana.

Finally, at about 1:30 p.m., he let the cat out of the bag, sort of: every applicant would have received a certified letter at the address on the application notifying them of the outcome—if they won, they'd be one of the twelve license permittees for the medical cannabis program. For us, that mailing address was in Newtown Square. And I immediately thought, *Lisa will be the one who received the letter.*

I leapt across the room in what felt like Superman taking flight as I reached for my cell phone. I pulled up my email first. All I remember clearly from that point on is seeing the subject line of Lisa's email, in all caps: WE WON!!!

Overwhelmed, I fell back on my bed and buried my head in a pillow. Tears of relief and excitement poured out of me. Wale did not even try to console me—he just let me cry into that pillow like he knew why I was crying! I must have cried for a few minutes, and I think Wale even managed to snap an embarrassing picture of me, tears streaming down my face.

I then called the CEO. We conferenced in Lisa and shared our joy.

We were one of just twelve medical cannabis grower-processor ventures in the state awarded a permit. Just about a week later, on June 29, the dispensary award winners were announced, and Ilera won again—one of twenty-five dispensary license award winners. That made us one of only five vertically integrated license winners— meaning we had permits to both supply and sell our product.

If you're a math mind, you'll appreciate the odds we faced: There were a few hundred businesses vying for the few precious permits to operate medical cannabis growing/processing facilities and dispensaries in just six regions of the state. The Department of Health received 457 applications in total, including 177 grower/processors and 280 for dispensaries.

The CEO wasted no time in extending an employment offer to me. On July 1, 2017, I officially became COO of Ilera Healthcare. And although I didn't get paid for any of my time since my at-risk offer in April, it didn't matter—I was happy as hell to be getting a paycheck again!

Even though I was elated, there was no time to celebrate. We still had enormous challenges to meet and faced extremely tight deadlines. Those fourteen- and sixteen-hour days weren't going to end anytime soon—they had only just begun!

Luckily, we weren't the only ones who wanted this project to succeed. Within a week of winning the license, we were flooded with calls from people who wanted to work with us. And in what would turn out to be a huge blessing for Ilera, one of those people was a man named Bill Palmer. Bill goes by the nickname "Wild Bill"—and Bill is *the Man*.

Bill had *everything* on lock. His construction company builds hospitals, factories, schools, churches, and more. Even better, Bill is from the Fulton County area, so he knew the territory *and* his job, inside and out. When he showed up at our very first construction meeting, he brought along no fewer than seventeen people. Everyone who would be involved in the project was represented. He brought architects, electricians, structural engineers, landscapers, plumbers, and subcontractors. He came in strong, had all the bases covered and was ready to go from day one.

What's more, Bill also worked at risk. He was very cognizant of the deadlines; he knew that the entire project balanced on a knife's edge of perfect timing. Once he came on board, things started to fall into place.

And it's a good thing they did: The state gave us just six months from licensing to be ready for an operations inspection by the Department of Health—six months to get everything built and ready to run! We had to construct a brand-new, 67,000-square-foot greenhouse and processing facility on virgin land, get the facility approved, and then build at least one of three dispensaries so we'd be ready to begin operations as a state-approved medical cannabis facility if approved. Only after the inspection and certification would we be allowed to move forward with cultivation. The grow facility alone was a vastly complex undertaking; it was like building a factory that also has a greenhouse attached to it. And the greenhouse is a very mechanically sophisticated system: a semi-closed loop with environmental controls that govern everything from watering and humidity to temperature and light and scores of other environmental factors. Then there are the work areas, including offices; conference areas; rooms for warehousing and packaging. There are also rooms for processing the plants—from drying to curing to extraction and infusion. To say that it was a lot to achieve in such a short time frame is a massive understatement, and we worked under the belief that *everything* had to be built *exactly* as we'd described it in our application, and within the state's strict time frame.

The smallest misstep, the tiniest miscalculation, would mean we'd lose our license . . . or at least, that's what we thought. We believed there would be absolutely no wiggle room, and so even when it became clear that a smaller facility would be much more feasible to build in such a tight time frame, we doubled down and forged ahead. If only we knew . . .

We took the state's deadline to heart, though, and I'm happy to say we met it. Some other licensees, however, did not—and as far as I know, were not penalized, either, which was *shocking* to me! Because when we were told six months, we took it as, "Be operational in six months at the risk of losing your license." By the time we broke ground, that left us just four and a half months to clear the virgin land and build the entire 67,000-square-foot facility—a monumental task that would take all the commitment, mental fortitude, and determination the team possessed.

In April, just after the applications were submitted, I was reviewing the paperwork and had a horrible thought:

If we won, six months would not be sufficient to become operational. The only way to pull this off would be to begin the work at risk. To be honest, I kept reading and rereading our application out of anxiety and anticipation, and trying to formulate a plan.

Among the many early challenges was finding out it was going to take a few months to get our state NPDES (National Pollutant Discharge Elimination System) permit, which would allow us to begin construction on our grow facility.

A preliminary survey had found we'd have to include a riparian buffer zone to protect a stream on the site. To further complicate matters, we learned that April to October is bat mating and roosting season in the Fulton County area. That meant no trees could be felled during that time period. Yet if we waited until we won the license—and our NPDES permit—we would not be allowed to disturb the trees, which meant we would not be permitted to build, which meant we could lose the license. Mind you, we had just locked down a virgin, sixty-acre piece of property. We knew there was no way we'd be able to clear trees from all sixty acres, then remove all the stumps to begin excavation and still meet our time line.

Now, because of the sensitivity of the cannabis issue, it was crucial that every step of the process was aboveboard. There were no corners to cut.

Because it was a brand-new program, the entire state had its eyes on the process. The Department of Health was watching all of the grower-processor license winners like a hawk. Yet it was also clear the DOH wanted the program to work, and that while they would be the regulators/custodians, they were also going to do everything they could to be partners in its success. We worked together closely, communicating with them almost every day, and they provided all the support we needed to succeed.

Meanwhile, the Ilera team was going over everything with a fine-toothed comb. We were ensuring all the bases were covered, down to the tiniest detail and the tiniest legality, ensuring we adhered to the operational process as outlined in our application. And in one of many proactive moves, our team came up with a creative solution to the bat mating issue.

It turned out that Department of Environmental Protection regulations would allow trees to be *cut* from November to March, but no earth could be disturbed until we had our NPDES permit. So, we hired a contractor to clear about thirty of the sixty acres our facility required, leaving the trees on the ground and the stumps intact. It was yet another gamble—we had no idea if we'd be awarded one of those twelve licenses.

During my first trip to the Fulton County site—pre-award—I found myself standing in the middle of a field surrounded by felled trees and stumps that came up to my knees. I remember thinking, "How are we going to pull this off? How will we transform this space into a usable grow facility in just six months if we win?"

And back then, I didn't even know about yet another challenge we'd face: The NPDES permitting process also required the project to go through a thirty-day public comment period before we could break ground. When we found out a few weeks after approval, the news was a little nerve-racking but it seemed doable—until we found out that we would have to wait at least *two business weeks* for the project plan to be published in the official *Pennsylvania Bulletin*—just one of the publications required for the thirty-day period. I thought to myself, *You gotta be kidding me!*

When all was said and done, we'd end up waiting almost forty-four days—until August 24—for the thirty-day public comment period to end. And we weren't going to waste a minute: We had planned an uneventful groundbreaking for that same day, at noon. What could have been a grand ceremony, if we'd had time, was instead going to be the first on-site contractors' meeting and commissioning of the site for work by local and state regulatory personnel.

Because the Pennsylvania Department of Environmental Protection knew how critical the timing was, they were prepared. On the morning of the 24th, they had the permit and all the documents we needed ready to go.

But there was one final challenge, at least for that morning: Their office is in Harrisburg, a sixty-eight-mile drive—136 miles round trip—from our site in Fulton County. They told me they couldn't release anything before 9 a.m., but I wasn't taking any chances. I was in the parking lot, nervously waiting, at 8:30 in the morning.

By 8:50 I was walking down the steps to their office, and when the door opened at 9, there it was: a giant pile of documents with Ilera's name on it. I hustled the package back to the car, said a quick prayer and—with apologies to any state troopers who might be reading this—I hauled ass back to the Fulton County site so that we could review everything and get started.

At just a few minutes past noon, with no reporters or state representatives, balloons, or fireworks, we broke ground to the roar of heavy construction equipment.

Now, any one of the challenges up to this point—the sixteen-hour days, the stress of not knowing if we'd get our license or our NPDES permit, or if I'd get paid—would be justification enough for someone to throw in the towel, or even end up sitting in the corner of a padded cell, rocking back and forth.

But in the midst of all this, I was hit with a bombshell phone call that nearly toppled my world. My mother started talking as soon as I picked up. "'Dare, your father is not doing well . . . Dr. Adebayo asked me to send you his test results. They said it could be really bad, and he needs medical attention immediately. His liver enzymes are high, and something called a PSA is also really high. . . . The doctor wants him to travel to you in America to see a specialist immediately."

I sank into my seat and honestly did not feel anything for a while. The world froze, and I was numb. It turned out my father very likely had an aggressive form of cancer, while he was simultaneously battling a potentially fatal liver disease.

And I found out just two weeks after we'd won the license.

CHAPTER 5

"What Was the Progress Today?"

After that initial call with Mom, I was reeling. I looked over the information she'd sent me, and the prognosis was grim.

To say I was in shock is an understatement. The call about my father had come two weeks after news that Ilera had won both licenses. I found myself experiencing two completely opposite emotions—elation and heartbreak—at the same time. It was surreal. It was like there was a halo of joy because we'd won, but then half of that halo had been snapped off under the weight of knowing my father could very well die.

I needed to shake myself out of it quickly, though. "The doctor is not optimistic," my mother had told me. "He's not comfortable with your father not immediately dropping everything and heading straight to get medical attention."

I pulled myself together and followed up on our phone call by sharing the test results with a doctor here in Philadelphia that my father had been coming to see since 2004 for treatments related to his liver function, which had long been affected by a childhood illness. "Get him here quickly," the doctor said. "This is not looking good." I immediately got to work on a plan, and the next few days were dedicated to making phone calls, getting opinions, and setting things in motion.

It was the last week in June, and Mom's birthday was coming up in the first week of July. I had a very eerie feeling from the discussions I'd been having with doctors, family, and friends about Dad. I was hoping for the best but wanted to be prepared for the worst. As part of that, I wanted to ensure my parents got to enjoy some time together.

I tried to keep my voice from breaking when I shared the doctor's recommendation with my mother. "We don't know what's coming next, but let's be strong," I said. "I made an appointment for Dad here, but it's not for another few weeks. Why don't you take the scenic route to the United States and spend a few days together, just the two of you, and celebrate your birthday. Then head here to the United States, and we'll begin the fight."

My brothers jumped in after that conversation, and we pulled together a great vacation package for our parents in Dubai. But we still had to persuade my father to take the trip. He was already resisting taking extra time off, and even wondering aloud why they weren't coming straight to see me. I asked my mother not to tell him how bad things looked, because he might not seek treatment if he knew things were dire.

But my mother, being the strong woman that she is, was able to persevere. Dad grudgingly agreed to a few days in Dubai. It was another bittersweet moment for me: I was elated to see them finally taking some time to enjoy themselves—but there was a feeling of hopelessness, too, at knowing this might be their last vacation. The fact that Mom's birthday was part of the trip gave us a guilt card to play against his resistance.

When they arrived at the Philadelphia International Airport, on July 8, I was shocked. You could *see* how sick my father was. He was so swollen his shoes wouldn't fit; Mom said he had to wear sandals all the time. His skin and eyes were discolored. He looked exhausted. My heart caught in my throat—his condition was even worse than I'd expected.

After we got home, I sat them down and broke the news about the gravity of the situation at hand. The three of us developed a plan of action. We needed to get other doctors' opinions and find a course of treatment. I laid it all out for Dad, and although he seemed skeptical, he grudgingly agreed, but he was not as combative as he was in Nigeria.

His first appointment here was set for late July, and it was a watershed moment for him. The doctor examined him, reviewed the test results, and then looked my father in the eye.

"Although we still need a definitive diagnosis from an oncologist, the numbers I am seeing here suggest that we may be dealing with an advanced stage of prostate cancer," he said. "I'll call my friend who is a urologist, and he would probably suggest that you go straight to the oncologist with these numbers."

The doctor picked up his phone and dialed his colleague, who confirmed almost verbatim what the doctor just said. My heart sunk in my chest, and out of the corner of my eyes I saw Dad take a deep breath.

Then he asked my father what *his* plan was. You could tell Dad did not completely grasp the gravity of the situation, and he was trying to paint a less grim picture. "Well, once I feel better, I'm going back home and going back to work," he replied.

The doctor didn't pull any punches: "Johnson,[1] with the numbers I'm looking at, especially with your liver, we have a lot of work ahead of us. I can assure you that if you go back to Nigeria right now, you are going to die."

I watched my father sink into his seat at the doctor's words. For the first time, the weight, the enormity, the monstrous *gravity* of what we were dealing with hit him. It's a very humbling thing, to see a parent in that situation.

---

1   Dad commonly used his middle name; his first name, Olusayo, could be challenging for some to pronounce.

I felt like my heart was going to break. He managed to hold himself together for the rest of the appointment, but by the time we got home, he was very emotional.

At first, my mother, father, and I gathered around the island in my kitchen—the center point of my town house. My father stood next to the refrigerator, and I was across from him. "What are we going to do?" my mother asked, her voice breaking. "We're going to figure this out," I told them both. "I'm going to take care of you."

My mother went downstairs at that point, and my father walked slowly to my couch and sat down. Then he put his head in his hands and wept. I realized then that neither of my parents wanted the other to see just how upset they were.

"Dad," I repeated, "I'm going to take care of you." And it was like that flipped a switch—his primary concern was suddenly not with his health, but with how I was going to cope with all the new challenges at Ilera!

"How exactly are you going to be able to do all that *and* care for me?" he asked. "How can you do all this?" But I just kept repeating myself and brought the focus back to him: "Don't worry about *that*, Dad. I'm going to take care of you. But you have to work with me. You have to trust me. You're going to be fine. With God's help, we will get through this."

And that made him cry even more.

Then I went to speak with my mother. "What are we going to do?" she kept asking me, between tears. "What are we going to do?"

I told her what I'd told my father. "With God's help, we will get through this," I said. "Just trust me. I *will* take care of Dad."

It was back and forth after that—I'd walk upstairs and talk with my father, then go downstairs and talk with my mother again. And neither wanted the other to hear their worry! It would have been comical, were it not for the severity of the situation.

Honestly, I had no idea how I was going to do it all. I realized I had two very serious responsibilities, and I refused to choose between them. It was going to be my job *and* my family. I was gripped with sadness and fear, but at the same time a determination was rising up inside of me. I was steeling myself for war. "I don't know how I'm going to pull this off; I don't know what the future holds," I said to myself, "but bring it on."

This was my father, after all; the man who had raised me. For him, and for my mother, I would do everything and anything. And I needed to make sure they *both* knew that. My mom had to go back to work in a little over two weeks. You could see the worry on her face—for Dad and for me. I knew she also needed reassurances that I could swing everything.

"I'll do whatever it takes," I told them both, when I finally had them together in the kitchen again. "We don't know what the future holds, and I don't know exactly *how* I will do it, but right now all you need to know is that I *will* do it. I will take care of you."

My father sat across the table from me. His hands were frail. His body was swollen. But he still had plenty of strength to shoot me a very stern look as I told them this. I was worried he'd reject it all; that he'd tell my mother they were going home, and our chance to save his life would be lost. But then I saw it: a glimmer of hope. There was just enough in his eyes to tell me, "Yes, we have a willing participant here." And for the first time since that initial call from my mom, I felt a little relief. He was going to avail himself for the fight ahead—and I'd won this first battle for all of us.

The next day, I called my youngest brother, who was driving. "Is Dad going to die?" he immediately asked me.

"Dad is gonna be fine," I replied. "There is no death sentence here, but he will not be coming home with Mom next week. I'm not going to lie to you, brother; this is serious. But he has as good a chance as any. And right now, we need to band together to get through this. You promise me that you boys will band together over there and take care of Mom. And I will take care of Dad."

At that point he lost it, and I had to tell him to pull over. Once he'd calmed down, I called my other immediate younger brother. Thankfully, he held it together— he'd always been one of the strongest in our family. I explained the situation to him and said, "You need to take care of Mom for me, so that I can concentrate on Dad." He promised he would—and he kept that promise, just as I kept mine.

* * *

From that day forward, the weeks blurred. I was in the thick of juggling everything related to meeting our time lines at Ilera, ranging from permit applications and regulatory approval deadlines with the Department of Health to managing organizational ramp-up, including hiring staff and attending to the operational readiness that goes into building a start-up.

At the same time, I was also in the thick of meeting my father's needs. He tried not to show it, but he was really feeling the effects of his combined health problems. He could barely walk. He had no energy. Everywhere we went, everything we did, he was just dragging.

To make matters worse, it often felt like we were just going from one doctor to another to another for a while. We'd visit a liver specialist here, an oncologist there, and then go to see his primary care physician—all to get a sense of what we needed to address first, what steps we needed to take next. It was exhausting—but my father went to every single one of the examinations and consults that I set up; he didn't offer any resistance.

Things looked worse with each consultation. We did our best, though, and took it one day at a time. And just when I thought we had a plan in place, we hit a roadblock. After a few appointments at a leading hospital in the area, we got a phone call. My father was an international patient, without traditional health insurance, and that had sent up red flags. "How are you going to handle paying for treatment?" the voice on the other end asked me. "By doing what I'm doing now, paying for each appointment as it comes, and then paying for the treatments as they come," I replied.

But the financial department categorically told us they would need about $150,000, up front, before they would go any further. They wouldn't even set another appointment. "I can't just write a check for $150,000!" I said. "I'd have to sell my house, and even then, that probably wouldn't be enough to cover it. But I *can* pay for individual appointments and treatments."

We were prepared for the financial burden—it wasn't even a question. My father was sick, and we were going to do whatever it took to get him well. But try telling that to a hospital's financial department. They flatly refused to treat Dad until they had *all* of the money in hand, or proof of funds that they could access—like an escrow account.

That setback cost us almost two valuable months, but we were able to switch to a different hospital system. I have to give a lot of credit to all the people who worked with us there. His personal physician, Dr. Gordon Ijelu, and his liver specialist, Dr. Eyob Fayesa, were nothing short of amazing. They treated my father not just as a patient, but as a human being, as an individual with feelings.

Furthermore, they understood the constraints we faced with my father's international status, and they worked with us so that we were able to manage the payments for his treatment. In fact, they went above and beyond: When Dr. Fayesa prescribed a medication that, out of pocket, would have cost us an astronomical *$14,000* a month, he wrote a letter to the manufacturer explaining our situation. The end result was an unexpected—and lifesaving—blessing: my father was able to use the drug free of charge.

* * *

It was a crazy, crazy time. If I wasn't taking my dad to the hospital for a consultation or test, I was in the middle of a call with my Ilera team, or I was reading up on regulations that dealt with construction permits or medical cannabis. I remember during some of Dad's MRIs, I would step out to join conference calls with our construction team while the machine clicked and whirred around him. We logged hundreds and hundreds of hours of conference calls in the span of about six months—and he logged a *lot* of MRIs and doctor visits.

And, of course, there were the trips—to Fulton County, where the grow facility was under construction; or to Harrisburg to meet with Department of Health officials; and the flights out to Denver, Las Vegas, and Los Angeles, the train rides to Baltimore, and Washington, D.C.—all cities that had previously established medical cannabis programs that we were studying. I was on the go constantly, just trying to stay on top of everything. The Fulton County drive alone was exhausting: I would leave Philadelphia at 5:30 in the morning to beat traffic, and I wouldn't return until after 10 p.m. Some nights I was so tired I'd stop several exits early in the suburbs to sleep in a hotel, because my GPS showed traffic was so backed up I'd still have another hour-plus to get to my home in South Philadelphia.

But despite the craziness, despite the uncertainty, despite the fear about my father's health, it was one of the best times of my life. Every night that I came home, whether it was from a drive to Fulton County, a weeklong trip across the country, or just from a long day of meetings, my dad was sitting there, waiting for me.

He always wanted to know how things were going. He would ask me, "What was the progress today?" The man would put his own pain aside and just be a father to me—his adult son. He recognized that I was juggling so much that, at times, I could barely keep everything in the air, and he managed to stay strong, to be my father, my friend, my confidant, through all of his own pain and anxiety. He remained all of that and more for me and for the entire family. He was a rock.

Mom, of course, was strong too. Every day she would call to check in on me and to check in on Dad. She prayed hard. Meanwhile, Dad and I would just go from one medical visit to another. With each we had a little more clarity, and by the time it was late August, we had a very clear understanding of what was going on with his liver and were ready to move forward with treatment for his prostate, too.

Mind you, he did not have a definite diagnosis of prostate cancer. For one thing, they couldn't do a biopsy because some of the blood markers related to proper clotting were way off. The doctor was afraid to stick Dad with a needle—if he developed a bleed, it would be internal, and they wouldn't be able to detect it. In short, the test itself could prove fatal. But all of his doctors agreed that he should begin treatment to slow his prostate's rate of growth—and we followed their advice to the letter.

What's more, my father began to make a round of *complete* lifestyle changes. He became personally empowered to take on his own health and wellness. He exercised daily. He agreed to change his diet. He read up on cancer and would ask questions about specific elements of his treatment.

It was astounding to watch Dad's transformation. A few years earlier, a hepatologist at Einstein Medical Center—the same doctor we were seeing now—had made recommendations my father had ignored. But this time he became very self-motivated to participate in his treatment plan—and that was half the battle. It made a huge difference, too. With each new test result, his numbers looked a little better. His liver function started to return to normal. His PSA levels dropped a bit. And our spirits lifted.

Then, in October, my sister-in-law came to stay with us. She was seven months pregnant and had a glow about her I cannot describe. She was such a fantastic addition to the household—brightening our moods and lightening my schedule. I'd been taking my father with me as much as possible when I traveled, but there were times I had to leave him at home. Now she was here to help keep him company, and she was of great help with taking care of Dad.

Dad seemed well on the road to recovery at this point, and the next two months flew by. He wasn't cured—they still did not even have a definitive diagnosis—but lifestyle changes and medication had his liver enzymes under control, and he was quickly returning to his old self: witty, funny, and so determined to catch up on work with his legal practice that he started meeting with them virtually.

Then, on December 5th, we had more great news: my sister-in-law had a healthy, nearly seven-pound baby boy.

The timing was perfect, in so many ways. There was the much-needed joy his birth brought to our family, of course. But all the while I'd been taking Dad to appointments and treatments, we'd been building Ilera's 67,000-square-foot grower/processor facility. And now, on the very same morning that the completed facility had received its certificate of occupancy, my nephew had been born. It felt like the hand of God at work.

We all agreed that one of his names needed to be Korede. In Yoruba, the word literally means "to arrive bearing blessings." And my nephew's arrival was symbolic of the coming together of so many joys and blessings: the joy of his birth, my father's improvement, and the progress we'd made to get the certificate of occupancy. To top it off, my sister told me Korede was already one of their top name contenders—in part because it also happens to be his father's middle name.

* * *

When I look back on that five-month experience, I cannot help but think that it was meant to be and that some part of this needed to happen. We certainly could all have done without the heartache and trouble we'd gone through. Yet I am especially grateful for the time I got to spend with my father, despite the circumstances. In the end, it brought our family even closer together—and taught all of us something about each other.

What did I learn in those five months?

1. I learned many of the reasons why, while I was growing up, that Dad was a father, and not necessarily a friend. He understood that raising four boys would require him to be a very present, very active, and sometimes very strict father. As a result, he and my mother raised four strong, successful men—men who, as boys, were often troublesome, but today are a band of brothers and a family of love.

2. I learned that my father still loved to learn, and he's proof that it's never too late to embrace something new and change your way of thinking. He became a student of his own health, but also a student of cannabis. He began to think differently and to ask questions about how the body reacts to cannabinoids and other compounds in the plant. He began to ask questions about the legal and social justice issues surrounding it; and he began to ask questions about its economic impact. He studied how this long-vilified plant could fit into the agricultural/medical space. He went from a man who'd always believed cannabis was an evil substance to a father who is very proud that I'm working to create medicines that can address a wide variety of conditions in people. He was so inspired, he even reached out to a friend in Nigeria; a college colleague who had lost his sight to glaucoma. After a long conversation with Dad and I, this man gained some clarity about how to treat his own condition and get the right medical help and was extraordinarily grateful for my father's call.

3. I learned that, as much as he looked forward to a full recovery, my father, ultimately, was looking forward to celebrating Ilera's success with me. And he was excited about going home and sharing what

he had learned about health and about medical
cannabis.

4. I learned that you are only as good as the options
    you put on the table. Our team firmly believed
    the only choices to consider were those that
    included a way to become operational in six
    months. Despite the enormous challenges of
    building a 67,000-square-foot facility and getting
    everything ready to go in that time frame, we
    were determined to make it happen. And it was
    the same with my father. The only options worth
    considering were those that led to his recovery.
    Giving up was not an alternative.

5. I learned that even the longest days are made
    shorter when someone who truly cares, someone
    who is truly engaged in your life, is there to
    remind you of your goals and ask, "What was the
    progress today?"

CHAPTER 6

Growing a Company from Seed

I decided to write this book because, as I've mentioned, I found myself at the intersection of divine providence and opportunity. I had happened to be a grad student in California, a state with a well-established medical cannabis program. I'd had a sleep-related disorder while there; I'd had the privilege of having people around me who pointed me in the right direction when traditional pharmacology failed me; and I'd had the opportunity to legally see a physician who made a medical cannabis recommendation that produced a very positive result. I also had the privilege to be a scientist who understood the repair that had taken place in my body. And I had the presence of mind to be able to contemplate what was going on not just within the context of my physiology, but on a wider scale: I could contemplate my socialization around cannabis and its legality, and beyond that I was able to see and to recognize opportunities to be in that space when Pennsylvania decided to begin their program.

I've talked about how we built the largest facility in the state dedicated to legally growing cannabis. I've talked about the permits we needed, and the hurdles we cleared to become operational. But I've been waiting to talk about one of our most important assets; something that's so critical we couldn't have achieved so much so quickly without it:

Our team.

A lot of people my age will say, "I want to get into the cannabis space," or "I want to get into a start-up." But when the rubber meets the road, reality is a lot different than expectation.

And forming not just a start-up, but a *cannabis* start-up, presents its own set of challenges. While we needed very specific, expert-level skill sets, we also needed to get the right people on our team. We needed not just knowledge-able people, but good people who would fit the culture at Ilera. We needed people who could buy into a vision, and (to borrow a term from author Jim Collins) take a seat on the *bus* of that vision, and be ready to ride it, with the team leaders, wherever it goes.

In a start-up, every turn could require you to jump, sprint, or slide—or a combination of all three—and you must be ready for whatever comes next. You need people who are flexible. You need people who can share your dream.

As a leader, in order to achieve a goal, you must first envision it; you must see how all the parts will come together to form the whole. If the team members don't share that vision; if they can't see what their leader sees, it's going to end up like the parable of the blind men and the elephant: each person will disagree about what the end result should look like.

That's a sure recipe for failure, or at least a catastrophe.

In April 2016, when I met the board's pick for CEO, Greg Rochlin, we invested a lot of time in understanding where our specific strengths were, and how our skill sets were complementary. I worked very hard to show my loyalty, to show "I am on this team. We are going to do this, whatever it takes." It was important to me that the CEO never had to worry about whether I'd have his back.

One of the things he'd often say is, "Team fit is very important. You need to work with people whom you like working with; people who don't care what their job description is on paper. If something needs to be done, they don't ask, or say 'That's not my job!' They just do it."

There's something very refreshing about that; about being able to rely on your team members to do what needs to be done, even if that's not their role on paper. We knew we were going to grow, and there would be clearer boundaries as we did. But at the moment, we were all pitching in. Even the CEO was down at the farm helping to set up—he moved around tables in the offices; he helped in setting up our dispensary; he pitched in wherever there was a need. That's almost unheard of for a CEO.

And that's the great thing about our team: You never heard anyone say, "It's not my job." When it was time for our first harvest, almost everyone—even from our Philly offices—was in scrubs helping out somewhere along the assembly line, to the point where we had to figure out staffing for other roles. Everyone there wanted to help—and it was so refreshing.

Very early on, as we started to build this team, we could quickly see the people who were the real gems, a genuine fit—and those who were more like cubic zirconia. On the surface, they looked great. Their résumés were top-notch; they interviewed well; but when it was time to do the actual work, it soon became apparent that they weren't up to par. And we wasted no time separating the imitations from the diamonds.

Which brings me back to Jim Collins and his book, *Good to Great: Why Some Companies Make the Leap . . . And Others Don't.*[1]

"Leaders of companies that go from good to great start not with 'where' but with 'who,' he writes. "They start by getting the right people on the bus, the wrong people off the bus, and the right people in the right seats. And they stick with that discipline—first the people, then the

---

1   Jim Collins, *Good to Great: Why Some Companies Make the Leap and Others Don't.* (New York: HarperBusiness, 2001), 35.

direction—no matter how dire the circumstances. Once you fill your bus with the right people in the right seats, it becomes less a question of where you're headed—and instead, how far you can go."

On our bus, we moved people around quite a bit—some into different seats, others into adjoining seats, and some into new, custom-built seats. On several occasions we made an unscheduled stop and removed people from the bus altogether. Take, for instance, one of our management roles—a seat we were certain we needed to have filled early on. The person we picked, however, turned out to be phenomenally better than her initial job description. We had to redefine the role we needed to fill, and her job now includes everything from helping out with cultivation to logistics. She was so much more versatile than her job requirements, and if we had limited her just to the initial role, we would really have missed out.

We had a similar experience with another phenomenal employee whom we eventually made our director of network engagement and physician engagement. We'd originally hired her to be more of a traditional physician sales representative, but we had to change her title, in part because her skills surpassed her original role. She managed our early marketing and literally executive-produced our path through the soft launch and the grand opening.

There were other roles that we changed as well, but it all boils down to the same thing: A lot of start-ups fail early on because they top-load. They are very heavy on high-paying management positions, but very light when it comes to roles related to actual business function and execution. In other words, they don't have enough boots on the ground and hands at the wheel.

We were determined not to do that at Ilera. We made flexibility a priority—if we saw someone was better suited for another role (or roles), we moved them into a different seat. We didn't rely on just résumés; we were careful to vet candidates to ensure they fit our culture and that personalities would mesh.

Interviewing an applicant can sometimes teach you a lot more about your organization and philosophy than about the person you're interviewing. On more than one occasion, that process yielded shifts in our thinking about a role we were trying to fill. It's a wonderful experience when you are thinking about a position or a need, and the person you're interviewing meets that need and more.

I had the privilege of hiring several department heads who reported directly to me. Looking back, most of them were value-added hires who brought so much more to the company than was outlined by their intended role.

And, of course, there were the times we needed to make tough decisions and let people go. I could write an entire chapter on that process; about the conflicting philosophies on how to dismiss an employee. Our CEO believed that you do it immediately—you don't delay the process or wait and hope things will magically improve.

Early on, he let a few people go, and there were questions about why he did it—even from me. When I asked him, he simply said, "When you feel that someone isn't a good fit, you don't drag it along."

In the years since, I have had conflicting thoughts about this strategy. And for every person we let go, I always wondered, "Was there something we could have done differently?"

While I agree that some situations call for showing an employee the door immediately, I have also learned that there can be a great value to investing more time, money, and energy in someone who's not meeting your expectations. Because sometimes, all they need is a little redirection or training to grow right along with your team.

And on any team—especially on one like ours—you need your key players to buy into the mission, and to be agile and ready to respond to anything, because at a start-up, things change by the second. You need thoughtful, energetic, responsive people; people who can be confident and smart enough to admit when they make a mistake, and then learn from it.

In short, you need people who can pivot.

CHAPTER 7

The Louisiana Purchase

Up to this point, the speed and trajectory of Ilera's growth had been nothing short of astonishing. We created a company, assembled a team, built a grow facility, constructed dispensaries, and had product on the shelves in a little over a year.

I was feeling energized by our accomplishments and was ready for another challenge—the same way I'd felt at Iroko. It felt like I was crushing it. I told the universe, "I'm ready for more!"

And just like that, the universe provided.

In the last week of October 2018, I received a phone call from Dr. Chanda Macias, owner of the National Holistic Healing Center in Washington, D.C., and the executive chair of Women Grow, a national organization focused on female leadership in the cannabis industry. We had been introduced by my cousin at a Women Grow meeting in Washington, D.C., and I quickly became their "little brother." Dr. Macias and her husband, Michael Bobo, were already respected names in the medical cannabis space and soon became my mentors. They had walked this path already to build National Holistic, and I could call them anytime and ask questions as we built Ilera. Dr. Macias knew our capabilities well.

"Southern University in Baton Rouge, Louisiana, is looking for a new operator for their medical cannabis license. I think Ilera would be a perfect fit," she said.

Almost immediately after I got off our call, my phone rang again. It was Ilera's CEO. "There's a good chance you'll be flying to Louisiana," he said. Dr. Macias had already given him the details—and if this was the right fit, he wanted in.

Things moved so fast from there that by the first week of November we had begun negotiations with the university to take over the grow license. And like the original Louisiana Purchase—the single largest acquisition of territory in US history—our buy-in would significantly alter the shape, size, and even the philosophy of Ilera.

To understand the significance of this deal, a little history lesson is in order, because Louisiana's approach to legalized medical cannabis is long and convoluted.

Back in 1978, some forward-thinking state officials drew up Act 725, which created the Marijuana Prescription Review Board. The act cleared medical cannabis for "use as a therapeutic drug" by cancer and glaucoma patients.

Act 725 also tasked the Department of Health and Human Resources with appointing five members to the board: four doctors and a pharmacist. It then instructed the secretary of the DOH to "contract with the National Institute on Drug Abuse for the receipt of cannabis pursuant to regulations promulgated by the National Institute on Drug Abuse, the Food and Drug Administration, and the Drug Enforcement Agency."

But the state's DOH never followed through and progress, to say the least, stalled.

In 1991, the now thirteen-year-old bill was pulled out, dusted off, and amended. Spastic quadriplegia was added to the list of conditions, and the DOH was instructed to create a framework for prescription and distribution by 1992.

It took them until 1994 to comply, and the rules still weren't comprehensive enough to provide patients with legal access. In theory, patients could get a prescription, but there was no way to fill it because cannabis could neither be cultivated nor dispensed.

In 2014, another medical cannabis bill was introduced to the Louisiana Senate Health Committee. This one covered the trifecta: prescribing, growing, and dispensing cannabis. But it failed, garnering six "nays" and just two "yeas."

Finally, in June 2015, HB 149 was signed, sealed, and delivered. It both legalized and made provisions for medical cannabis—but in keeping with the state's conservative approach to date, it eventually granted just two licenses to grow, process, sell, and research medical cannabis. One went to Louisiana State University, and the other to Southern.

Now, while the Creole state might be behind the times in the number of licenses it granted, it's a solid step ahead in terms of what those licenses allow: *true clinical research.*

What's more, it puts one of those licenses in the hands of the very people who've arguably suffered the most under the war on drugs: Southern University is a histori- cally Black college.

After reviewing multiple bids for the project, Southern contracted with a privately owned company, Advanced Biomedics, to build and operate a medical cannabis grow facility. The university would handle the clinical research side of things, and together, they'd create new medicines.

Or at least, that was the plan. A year into the process, Advanced found that it couldn't deliver on its promises. The project was in jeopardy, and something had to be done, quickly.

By now, a number of university stakeholders had made it very clear that they wanted to work with Dr. Macias.

Dr. Macias had already established a reputation as a pivotal player in the national medical cannabis space, in terms of business acumen, clinical know-how, oper- ational excellence, advocacy, and her impact on social justice issues—and the stakeholders were impressed with what they'd heard and seen. Additionally, the university as a whole was wary of additional delays and setbacks, so the key players wanted a company that had already established itself in the field.

To facilitate our partnership with Southern, then, a new and distinct entity was formed. To name this new entity, we took the name Ilera, from Ilera Healthcare, and Holistic, from Dr. Macias's National Holistic, to create Ilera Holistic, a Louisiana-only entity that would manage the university's cannabis research program.

Yet this was in no way a sure thing. Hearing about a company and its principals is one thing, but we still had to pass muster under close inspection.

There were, of course, meetings upon meetings upon meetings. We discussed Ilera's strategy, our current facilities, the expertise of our team, and the success of our growers. We talked about the therapies we intended to create and those we'd already formulated. We talked about the challenges we'd surmounted and how those would apply to the challenges this project faced.

Yet our trip to Southern was about more than technical know-how and achievements: It was about Ilera's philosophy and culture. It was about *why* we do what we do, just as much as it was about *how* we do it. In order to determine that, the university's officials wanted to spend some time getting to know us better. And so, shortly into the trip, I found myself changing my Thanksgiving plans.

I'd intended to travel to Chicago to be with friends and family, but—at the request of Southern's board of trustees and board of supervisors—Dr. Macias and I were invited to spend the holiday "the Louisiana way." We soon found ourselves in New Orleans, guests at the table of one of our team-members-to-be in the midst of one of the biggest Thanksgiving celebrations in the nation.

Now, one of the staples of a Louisiana Thanksgiving is the Bayou Classic: the annual college football game between the Southern University Jaguars and the Grambling State University Tigers. But it's more than just a game—it's a two-day extravaganza.

And it felt like the entire Southern University community lives 363 days a year prepping for those two days. People fly from all over the country to be a part of that experience. There are fan and fitness festivals, a battle of the bands, a BizTech Challenge, luncheons, a parade, and of course, countless parties.

No matter where we went, each time our hosts introduced us, we were treated like celebrities. People knew we were two of Ilera's key players; they knew what we were there to accomplish. And they'd say to us, "you're giving us hope, you're giving us pride, and you're giving us inspiration."

To be among the Southern University community in my capacity with Ilera, and as an African American, was simply priceless. At one point, I was lying in bed trying to sleep, but my mind was going a mile a minute. I kept thinking, *Wow, is this happening? Is this* really *happening?*

In short order, a strategic decision was made: Rather than put the program at further risk, Ilera Holistic would come on board as the operating partners. This allowed the university to meet the license obligations and keep the program in operation.

By November 14, we'd concluded the deal. In just short of five weeks, we had developed the right partnership and gained the support of all the stakeholders. In a little over a month, we had become a multistate operation.

We were now positioned to operate one of just two medical cannabis licenses in Louisiana. In terms of the business, things got interesting very quickly. We were on a trajectory for a major victory.

Our clinical license made Southern the *first* historically Black university to hold a major medical cannabis license. This was a landmark moment, representing a step forward in the fight for racial equity in the cannabis industry. Both the historic and practical implications were enormous. A CNN story summed it up like this: "In theory, that puts Louisiana—and the two companies with exclusive licenses—in an excellent position to develop a repository of proprietary therapeutic compounds that could prove lucrative if the drug were ever legalized on a national level."[1]

---

1   Lydia DePillis, "Louisiana Is Trying to Keep Medical Marijuana Medical. It's Harder Than It Sounds," CNN Health, November 27, 2018, https://www.cnn.com/2018/11/27/health/louisiana-medical-marijuana/index.html.

For me, though, the most exciting component of all this was (and still is) the fact that we now held a true clinical research license, at least at the state level. This was a major leap in the right direction; a watershed event that would advance both our collective understanding of cannabis and the future of cannabinoid-based medicines and therapies.

Up until then, clinical research and therapeutic development in the United States had been possible only at the University of Mississippi, because they have a contract with the National Institute on Drug Abuse to grow cannabis. If you wanted to do any clinical research on cannabis, you had to go through the DEA and use outdated government-owned strains.

This deal and the structure of the Louisiana license was a game changer. Now we could form a partnership between academics and industry to create a range of new medications at the state level, while still respecting the federal prohibition.

Yet there's a personal victory in all of this, too. The partnership with Southern University is allowing me to realize my life's dream: to be a true translational scientist and accelerate the conversation between academia and industry, bringing treatments and therapies to patients faster.

And to accomplish all this with the *first historically Black university to hold a medical cannabis license in the country* just blew my mind. It's such a unique opportunity and such a unique set of circumstances that—at the risk of sounding clichéd—I'm still pinching myself to find out if it's all been just a dream.

CHAPTER 8

On Hope

What would you do if your child had a disorder that left him, literally, speechless?

If your son had daily meltdowns—sometimes more than one—that lasted up to three hours, and sometimes led to him harming himself or others?

If he became so overwhelmed by his emotions that he threw himself on the floor, shrieking, crying, and kicking over furniture?

Now imagine that the accepted range of medicines prescribed by your health professional to manage these symptoms causes a host of side effects, including loss of appetite, crankiness, constipation, insomnia, stomach pain, dizziness, slow heart rate, low blood pressure, and an increased risk of suicide and depression.

Would you accept the healthcare status quo?

Not if you're Erica Daniels.

Erica is a single mom, a pioneer,[1] a superhero,[2] and the founder of Hope Grows for Autism. She has guts, determination, intelligence, and a deep, unflinching love for her children—one of whom has severe autism. And after thirteen years of the status quo, Erica, fed up, decided to take her son's treatment into her own hands.

Like many parents of children with autism, Erica knew something was different about her son, Leo, very early on. But no one knew quite what.

Then, at nineteen months, Leo caught one of those childhood bugs that every kid suffers through—only Leo's lasted about twelve *weeks*. Over the course of those weeks, doctors placed him on round after round of antibiotics, but nothing worked. His body racked by high fevers, Leo was inconsolable.

Near the end of the illness—Leo was now twenty-one months old—Erica says she had a revelation. "I was holding Leo, trying to soothe him, and he began tapping on my shoulder in a repetitive manner. At that moment a light went off in my head and I thought, *autism*. Three weeks later, Leo was formally diagnosed."

Visits with pediatricians and specialists all over the country led to an ever-increasing list of treatments, therapies and, of course, pharmaceuticals. Doctors prescribed stimulants, blood pressure medications, anxiety

---

1   I'll get to that.
2   I'll get to that, too.

medications . . . yet nothing helped Leo much. In fact, most seemed to make his symptoms *worse.*

Adding to these challenges, Leo was also wrestling with food sensitivities, digestive issues, and even life-threatening food allergies.[3]

"He had issues with constipation. His GI issues worsened. He wasn't sleeping. He was crawling out of his skin, he was so uncomfortable," Erica says. "I was at a point of last resort, which is unfortunate, and which is where most autism parents get: I was at the point where I was considering a residential facility for him. He was having meltdowns almost five days a week. It could be for two or three hours; it could be for thirty minutes. Yelling, screaming, kicking—just stuck, and not able to get past."

Having read about cannabis-based therapies for autism, Erica started down an even deeper research rabbit hole that, eventually, led her to a trusted black-market supplier. "I left with a cartridge of cannabis oil—a strain called "Girl Scout Cookies"[4]—and I took a toothpick with a *teeny* drop, and that's how we started. And for the first time, Leo actually sat next to me on the couch and watched a movie with me."

---

3 The wrong ingredients can send Leo into anaphylactic shock. Erica literally has to monitor everything her son eats or drinks. I told you she's a superhero.

4 Girl Scout Cookies is a THC-dominant cannabis cultivar that also contains CBD and other minor cannabinoids.

It was such a profound difference; it was almost like night and day. He wasn't stimming.[5] He wasn't having a two-hour meltdown. He wasn't racing from one thing to the next.

"When I first tried using cannabis on him, I was very nervous about it, for a variety of reasons. But I had really never seen anything that worked so quickly and so dramatically, without any side effects other than him being tired if I gave too big of a dose. So, I knew I was on to something," Erica says.

But the cannabis oil wasn't just fast-acting. It was also far more effective at allowing Leo to function than anything they'd tried before. "In the first month of using the oil, he went down to having *one meltdown in thirty days*," she says, a note of awe still evident in her voice.

Erica was sold. Unfortunately, she couldn't get the medicine she needed in Pennsylvania—at least, not legally. She also wasn't willing to risk continuing to buy her son's medicine on the black market. So, once again bucking the status quo, Erica hopped a flight to Colorado[6] to visit a grower/processor that had developed a cannabis-based medicine for autism. She visited the lab, read the reports, met the pharmacist—and came home with a supply of life-changing medicine.

---

5   "Stimming" is any of a number of self-stimulating behaviors, usually involving repetitive movements or sounds. Examples include hand-flapping, pacing, clapping, rocking, excessive blinking, repeating noises, and more.

6   Her trip was documented in the "Herb for Autism" episode of the VICE show *Weediquette*.

From there, Erica developed a system with others in the group *MAMMA* (Mothers Advocating Medical Marijuana for Autism) to get cannabis-based medicine for their kids. "Our group of moms would take turns, and we'd each take trips—Colorado, Maine, California," she says.

That bridged the gap until Pennsylvania's clinics were up and running, but it was nerve-racking. Even though the women carried Safe Harbor letters—which, in practice, allowed them to transport their kids' medical cannabis—they were still taking a big risk by moving a federally illegal Schedule 1 controlled substance across multiple state lines.

All the while, Erica was doing her homework. In the early days of Pennsylvania's program, she was part of two medical cannabis license applications, both with the intention of developing a specific formula targeted at relieving the symptoms of autism. But the experience left a bad taste in her mouth.

One company failed to gain approval; the other was sold almost immediately after it gained its license. And even though a commitment was made to develop autism medication and to support nonprofit work and education in the autism field, "I quickly realized that autism was no longer going to be of interest to them," Erica says. "So I completely separated myself from that company."

"For a while, that was very discouraging. It was really tough to trust anyone, to find any grower who was interested in making an investment in what was probably the smallest patient population in the state.

"Then I found Ilera, and they were a much better fit and had exactly the same vision as I did," she says.

* * *

I first heard about Erica in June 2018, when I got an email from Melissa Jacobs, then the associate editor of the Philadelphia-area magazine *Main Line Today*. Melissa focuses mostly on health-related issues, and we'd already done several interviews regarding Ilera and medical cannabis.

The gist of her email was that she would like me to meet Erica and Brooke, two Philadelphia Main Line[7] moms who had come out very publicly about using cannabis to treat their sons. She shared that because the Pennsylvania program was so new, they were getting their medicines from out of state through the Safe Harbor Act, and they wanted to speak to someone local who could possibly help.

Then she introduced me by saying I was one of the savviest people she'd interviewed in the medical cannabis space, and that I was exploring some indication-specific

---

7   The Main Line is an informally delineated region that historically has been home to Philadelphia's wealthiest families. It encompasses 18 communities, including Gladwyne, Villanova, Radnor, Bryn Mawr, and Ardmore.

targets. She wondered if my work could benefit the autism community.

That single email set Hope (our proprietary formulation targeting specific cluster symptoms associated with autism spectrum disorder) in motion.

I remember my first meeting with Erica and Brooke so clearly. As soon as they walked into our conference room, I could feel the energy change. I could *feel* their apprehension. Erica's attitude was very reserved, very business-like—she was not overly friendly.

I was puzzled at first. After all, they had requested the meeting. But I quickly came to understand the reason for the tension. Because of Erica's prior experience with other medical cannabis players, she'd become very skeptical of the industry, and rightly so.

After we exchanged pleasantries, Erica told me her and Leo's story. Then she looked me in the eye and asked where autism spectrum disorder fit into Ilera's priorities. Erica explained that she was looking for a partnership, not just a supplier. She didn't want to help just her son; she wanted to help *all* ASD families—and I could tell she was ready to shake hands and walk away if that meeting didn't meet her expectations.

I was the only man in the room that day. I'd brought two members of my staff with me: both women, both mothers. And I think that's part of the reason we made so much progress. As I watched, I saw that negative energy change: The conversation soon went from the issues of running a business and understanding the development of formulations to a conversation with much more of a familial and parental connection. And as I observed, even I was transformed by the sheer will of these two mothers who would stop at nothing in their search for solutions for their children. I can tell you that it was not long after that initial meeting that ASD rose, very quickly, to the top of my priority list.

Pennsylvania, by law, had given us seventeen (now twenty-three) conditions for which we could create cannabis-based medicines—including ASD.

But on this day, my focus was on just one question: What is autism spectrum disorder?

I determined, in that moment, to find out everything I could about it. After our meeting, I immediately poured myself into devouring as much ASD research as I could, as quickly as I could. I read on flights, I read before bed. . . . I studied the available research every chance I got. And so, I became very consumed, between sometime in July 2018 all the way through September, immersing myself in research on ASD and its many manifestations.

Perhaps one of the most important things I learned: There is no one type of autism. That's why it's called autism *spectrum* disorder: the type and severity of symptoms varies from patient to patient.

While Erica's son, Leo, was essentially nonverbal, others with ASD have little trouble using language to communicate. Some ASD children, like Leo, are prone to hours-long meltdowns—emotional overloads, really—which often involve screaming, yelling, kicking, and hitting. Others have shorter, more subdued meltdowns; still others have short, yet very intense, meltdowns. The symptoms and expressions of ASD vary—from patient to patient, and, as some parents will tell you, from day to day and hour to hour.

The National Institutes of Health[8] calls Autism Spectrum Disorder a *"developmental disorder that affects communication and behavior. Although autism can be diagnosed at any age, it is said to be a "developmental disorder" because symptoms generally appear in the first two years of life."*

A 2014 study[9] by the CDC shows that, in the United States, about 1 out of 59 children has ASD; the World Health Organization estimates that globally, 1 out of 160 children has ASD. (At first glance, the disparity in numbers seems to point to a higher prevalence of ASD in the United States, but those numbers are likely due to reporting *and* recording discrepancies—we're focusing on ASD much more heavily here in the United States than in many other countries.)

---

8   National Institute of Mental Health, "Autism Spectrum Disorder," accessed August 18, 2019, https://www.nimh.nih.gov/health/topics/autism-spectrum-disorders-asd/index.shtml.

9   Gigen Mammoser, "Here's the Big Reason That Autism Rates Have Increased Again," Healthline, May 1, 2018, https://www.healthline.com/health-news/the-big-reason-autism-rates-increased-again#Behind-the-dramatic-increase.

ASD is diagnosed in boys four times more often than in girls; it occurs among all ethnic, racial, and economic groups; and it is a lifelong disorder. According to the American Psychiatric Association, people with ASD have symptoms that impair their ability to function properly in school, work, and other areas of life. They often have difficulty communicating and interacting with others. In some cases, that might be relatively mild—like a child who doesn't talk much, prefers to play alone, and appears awkward in group settings. In other cases, it may be more severe, and the simplest change in routine can trigger extreme anxiety and outbursts.

One of the challenges to treating the symptoms of ASD is that, unlike other diagnoses, it is an umbrella term. If, for instance, your child is diagnosed with strep throat, the doctor knows exactly how to treat it: antibiotics. But a diagnosis of ASD is really just a starting point. Experts previously used separate terms like Asperger syndrome; pervasive developmental disorder—not otherwise specified (PDD-NOS); and childhood disintegrative disorder (CDD) to describe different levels, if you will, of autism. But in 2013, the *Diagnostic and Statistical Manual of Mental Disorders 5* folded Asperger syndrome, PDD-NOS, and CDD into a blanket diagnosis of ASD.

Those with Asperger syndrome were often said to have a "mild" form of autism. The individuals are usually very bright, but socially awkward. They may have speech patterns that seem robotic, or at least different; they often have great focus and persistence but usually have limited interests, and suffer from hypersensitivities to smells, tastes, noise, or light; poor conversation skills; and anxiety and depression.

Similarly, PDD-NOS was used to describe someone with relatively mild or singular autism symptoms; for instance, serious deficits in social and language skills, but no other traits, such as meltdowns, stimming, or limited interests.

Childhood disintegrative disorder occurs when a normally developing child suddenly and sharply regresses. They lose language skills, motor skills, social skills, cognition and more.

To further muddy the ASD waters, people on the spectrum usually have other conditions to contend with as well, like Leo's food challenges. According to The National Autism Association's fact sheet, *"Comorbid conditions often associated with autism include Fragile X, allergies, asthma, epilepsy, bowel disease, gastrointestinal/digestive disorders, persistent viral infections, PANDAS, feeding disorders, anxiety disorder, bipolar disorder, ADHD, Tourette Syndrome, OCD, sensory integration dysfunction, sleeping disorders, immune disorders, autoimmune disorders, and neuroinflammation."*

All of this makes a one-size-fits-all treatment impossible, which is why patients are often prescribed multiple medications. It isn't uncommon for a child like Leo to take four or more different types of medications at once.

Among the most commonly prescribed are antipsy-
chotics, such as risperidone and aripiprazole; SSRIs such
as fluoxetine, fluvoxamine, sertraline, and citalopram;
non-SSRI anti-depressants venlafaxine and clomipramine;
stimulants including amphetamine, dextroamphetamine
and methylphenidate; anticonvulsants like sodium val-
proate, phenytoin, clonazepam, and carbamazepine . . .
and that's not including the list of drugs used to treat any
comorbid conditions, like ADHD, epilepsy, insomnia,
and gastrointestinal issues.

To make matters worse, as I mentioned earlier, all of
these medications can have serious (and in several cases,
long-lasting) side effects—some of which mimic the very
symptoms they're designed to treat!

The more I learned, the more determined I became
that we could produce safe, effective, cannabis-based
treatments. (Much has been written about the effects of
cannabis in the treatment of ASD, but that is a subject for
another book.) I knew, for instance, that studies coming
out of other parts of the world had shown blends of CBD
and THC oils held promise as a treatment for some of
the ASD cluster symptoms. But I was up against a serious
challenge. Due to the long-standing prohibition against
cannabis, there was a limit to the scientific data, long-
term medical studies, and conventional clinical trials that
we could rely on to formulate treatments.

Meanwhile, Erica and I had several conversations on our
own—though I'd already gone straight to my management

team and made a case for why we should work with her. My reasoning: As a company, part of our mission is to support or add to the body of available research by delving into aligning formulated products to very specific therapeutic conditions, not only to where the research was emerging, but also to where we could contribute to that research. That science sits at the core of our scientific engagement at Ilera Healthcare. We should be constantly reviewing the science that's available and seeing where it can help direct or guide our product development strategy.

To my joy, management didn't take much convincing. That led to a series of meetings with Erica, who was still very wary. It took weeks of continued conversations, in which she wanted to know about me and my scientific background, and about our company. We even had her meet core members of the team, all to help her understand that we were serious.

At one point, I said, "Erica, you showed up at our doorstep. I did not come looking for you. Although I knew that someday we would be pursuing indication-specific therapies, to be honest, I didn't think it would be this soon, or in this manner. But your experience is so compelling, and your courage and the courage of the families you represent so inspiring, that you've created a moral impasse for me where doing nothing is not an option. I can no longer go to bed at night without thinking about how I can help you and the autism community in Pennsylvania."

It was my way of saying, "It's too late to turn back now. Let's talk through the issues, and let's get started. I cannot unhear what I have heard or unsee what I have seen." I felt like she dropped a bomb on our doorstep. I felt like, "OK, you rocked my world, and we've shown you everything we can, so let's just cut to the chase and get started." It had gone from something that was simply work-related to something that was deeply personal.

I mean, it blew my mind that the medical cannabis program had existed in Pennsylvania for *over a year*, yet parents still had to go out of state to find medical cannabis solutions for their families! And that, then, became a burden of mine. I was feeling guilty that the program, for which I am a major player, was built on the backs of parents and advocates who stood on the front lines on behalf of their wards. Because when you look at the history of medical cannabis, it exists because of parents like Erica; parents who had the courage to advocate for their children suffering with epilepsy, autism, and other debilitating conditions; parents who fought to get the program into existence.

Yet when the licenses were awarded, those conditions did not get frontline focus from the medical cannabis industry—even though in states like Pennsylvania, those conditions were among the first to be approved for treatment with medical cannabis!

There is truth and strength in being completely vulnerable. I understood the path that Erica had taken to get here—she had been kicked from promise to promise, yet she pushed and fought through all of that to get to us. I could not relate to her pain and her journey, but the least I could do was come alongside her with my truth, without setting unrealistic expectations.

There is no cure for autism spectrum disorder. And I was in no position to say, "Here comes the silver bullet, let's wait." But I *was* willing to step up, stand beside her, and say, "How do we work together?"

Finally, because I had worked so hard to prove my sincerity, to feel comfortable, we came to a place where Erica realized she could work directly with me—she didn't need a go-between. You could feel the difference in the air between us; that initial resistance had melted away, and we were ready to move forward.

Before long, we were walking side by side on a journey to cocreate cannabinoid-based solutions that, we hoped, would address some of the cluster symptoms associated with ASD.

Osagie conceptualized a strategy to work within the prohibition on research, which in itself could take up an entire book. That solution gave birth to our launch, learn, and develop (LLD) strategy, which now is the basis of our development and rapid commercialization of cannabinoid-based medicines at Zelira Therapeutics.[10] LLD is a three-phase approach designed to rapidly bring new

---

10 The Australian-based biopharmaceutical company where I serve as Global MD and CEO. www.Zeliratx.com.

products to market while simultaneously gathering feed-back used to improve those products. The three phases can be described like this:

1. **Launch:** We focus on quickly and efficiently bringing the product to market. That includes science-backed product development, obtaining regulatory approvals where appropriate, and building a sales and marketing team.
2. **Learn:** We focus on gathering feedback from patients using the product that will be used to make improvements.
3. **Develop:** We focus on the product improvements, which may involve making changes to features, functionality, or marketing. We focus on quickly and efficiently gathering feedback from patients.

By October, Erica and I were standing on the precipice of something far bigger than I had ever imagined.

And as I reflect on these experiences now, I can see several of the lessons I learned:

1. Vulnerability is not optional.
2. Know your truths.
3. Be intentional about what you can do, today.

There's a beauty in assembling something, in combin-ing all these elements, without knowing what the output could look like. I didn't know exactly where the journey would take us, but I was ready to see it through. Because when I started working with Erica, all I saw in her was the hope she represented—not just for her son, but for children, parents, and caretakers all over the world.

Today, two white papers have been released detailing numerous ASD symptom improvements when patients used Hope 1 and/or Hope 2, formulas that came out of that initial collaboration.[11,12] Hope 1 and Hope 2 are among the most sought-after cannabis-based ASD medicines on the market, and Zelira Therapeutics is beginning FDA clinical trials of cannabis-based ASD treatments.

And our work in that space is only just beginning.

11 Thomas, M., et al. "HOPE 1 demonstrates improvements in clinical global impression (CGI) in patients with autism spectrum disorder." https://zeliratx.com/wp-content/uploads/2022/04/ZEL040-White-Paper_Hope_FA.pdf. Published March 2022. Accessed May 26, 2023.
12 Zelira Therapeutics. "Autism patients report improvement in symptoms and quality of life with Zelira Therapeutics' HOPE." https://zeliratx.com/presentations/HOPE/HOPE%20Patient%20Survey_WhitePaper%20(2019).pdf. Published June 2020. Accessed May 26, 2023.

CHAPTER 9

Numbers Don't Lie

There was an opinion piece in a November 2017 edition of the *Wall Street Journal* titled "Can Marijuana Alleviate the Opioid Crisis?"[1] written by Dr. Richard Boxer, a clinical professor at UCLA's David Geffen School of Medicine, and it really got me thinking.

It tells the story of a woman named Jennifer, a thirty-seven-year-old schoolteacher from Virginia who suffers from a genetic spinal disease that caused so much pain she could no longer work.

Jennifer, like millions of others across the country, had been prescribed opioids to alleviate the pain. But she wasn't satisfied. She knew they'd provide just limited relief, and that they came with a high risk of addiction—a risk she didn't want to take.

---

1   Richard Boxer, "Can Marijuana Alleviate the Opioid Crisis?," *WSJ* Opinion, Nov. 19, 2017, https://www.wsj.com/articles/can-marijuana-alleviate -the-opioid-crisis-1511104543.

Frustrated, Jennifer took matters into her own hands and went searching for alternative treatments. She settled on medical cannabis—which, at the time, was not yet legal in Virginia (the state has since approved the medicinal and responsible adult use of cannabis in a number of forms).

Jennifer drove to Washington, D.C., and visited three medical cannabis dispensaries, where she finally found a much better solution to ease her pain—with fewer side effects than any of the previous medications she'd tried. It gave her a new lease on life, and a new outlook on medical cannabis.

I've heard so many stories like this, about people who, like Jennifer, are at the end of their wits with the conventional medicines they've been prescribed—medicines that are considered acceptable because they've been approved by the FDA for prescription use, even though they are highly addictive and easily misused. Did you know that in 2016, more Americans—64,070—died as a result of drug overdoses than were killed in the entire Vietnam War?[2] More than 40 percent of those deaths were from *prescription* opioids such as fentanyl and tramadol. And this is considered acceptable by mainstream medicine.

Meanwhile, according to the CDC, there has never been a single cannabis overdose death—not one! Yet because of archaic laws, we had very limited access to research the

---

2   Ashley Welch, "Drug Overdoses Killed More Americans Last Year than the Vietnam War," CBS News, October 17, 2017, cbsnews.com/news/opioids-drug-overdose-killed-more-americans-last-year-than-the-vietnam-war/.

medical potential of cannabis, even in states where it had been legalized for medical use. Thankfully, in 2021, the DEA started to relax its grip on cannabis research, and since we started this book has amended its regulations and expanded the number of DEA-approved facilities permitted to grow cannabis used in research purposes.

But nonetheless, cannabis is still being called the "gateway drug"; people still talk about it in terms of addiction, addiction, addiction, addiction . . . but is that really a problem when we think about cannabis? Is it really an addictive drug, or is it being described that way in the shadow of truly addictive drugs that we understand, like opioids?

In Jennifer's case, she was simply trying to manage chronic pain so she could continue teaching. Her doctor gave her two choices: suffer through the pain or take conventional (and not very effective) prescription opioids that could leave her dependent on painkillers—or dead. Why are these acceptable options when there's a much safer third choice?

Consider this fact from the National Institutes of Health: From 1999 to 2010, states with medical cannabis laws saw a 24.8 percent lower mean annual opioid overdose mortality rate when compared with states that don't have medical cannabis laws.[3]

---

3   Bachhuber, M. A., B. Saloner, C. O. Cunningham, and C. L. Barry, "Medical Cannabis Laws and Opioid Analgesic Overdose Mortality in the United States, 1999–2010," National Library of Medicine, accessed April 17, 2019, www.ncbi.nlm.nih.gov/pubmed/25154332.

These are statistics from a *government* agency, not numbers made up by a shady drug dealer in an alley. Which begs the question: If we have this kind of evidence, what are we waiting for? A 24.8 percent drop in opioid deaths is enormous—and that's from fewer than forty states!

Now, in the time since we started this book, additional studies have given us new information to assess. And the COVID-19 pandemic caused a major uptick in opioid abuse, throwing a huge variable into the mix.

But the point remains that in places where medical cannabis is legal, hospitalization rates of people suffering from painkiller abuse dropped 23 percent, and rates of overdose requiring hospitalization dropped 13 percent. In Colorado, where they legalized medical cannabis in 2000 and recreational cannabis in 2012, they've experienced a 6.5 percent reduction in opioid-related deaths.[4] The numbers go on and on and on . . . and they don't lie.

Jennifer could easily have become an opioid statistic. To prevent that, she had to take matters into her own hands—and risk arrest—when she decided, "I'm not going to die like this." And now she's a medical cannabis advocate, and she's probably thinking, *Where do I fit into all of this? I just wanted a safer option to manage my condition, and now I'm at the center of a national debate.*

---

4   Melvin D. Livingston, Tracey E. Barnett, Chris Delcher, and Alexander C. Wagenaar, *Recreational Cannabis Legalization and Opioid-Related Deaths in Colorado, 2000–2015*. National Library of Medicine, accessed 26 February 2022, https://www.ncbi.nlm.nih.gov/pmc/articles/PMC5637677.

Ideologically, it seems everyone wants to argue cause and effect as a reason to keep cannabis illegal, but to do this, they're using false data and lumping cannabis use in with opioid addiction and mortality rates. If we look at the actual numbers, though, we find just the opposite is true. There's good reason to believe that the decriminalization of cannabis is linked to reduced opioid overdose, reduced opioid abuse, and reduced opioid-related deaths. As scientists, we need the freedom to study this, in a regular clinical drug trial.

I feel bad for people like Jennifer. They are not trying to commit a crime; they are not trying to break federal law. Instead, they are going the accepted route by trying every opioid their doctors prescribe. And despite risking addiction, they are still not finding relief. Frustrated, they look for other options—and when they eventually try cannabis, it's like a light bulb goes off: "Aha! This is so much more effective, and so much safer, and it's not what I expected at all!"

People like Jennifer are the reason I remain grounded and focused; it's why our work in the cannabinoid space is so important. We need to be able to research and create cannabinoid alternatives to the current crop of addictive, deadly and medically accepted opioids that claim thousands of lives every year.

Jennifer did not choose the genetic disease that causes her pain. She just wants to manage the pain in a way that is not addictive. But if we don't allow scientists the freedom to thoroughly study cannabis; if we as a nation continue to prohibit it like we've done for so many years, are we doing people like Jennifer a favor?

Or are we handing them a death sentence?

CHAPTER 10

Racism and the War on Drugs: Sowing the Seeds of Discontent

"Cannabis" or "marijuana?"

Today, it's generally accepted that the words are an umbrella term for the cannabis plant and most of its products—both medicinal and recreational (what I prefer to call responsible adult use).

Way back in 1753, Swedish botanist Carl Linnaeus classified the *Cannabis sativa* plant. In 1785, French biologist Jean-Baptiste Lamarck classified another, the *Cannabis indica* plant. Now, there's much more to cannabis than just those two designations, but that's a subject for another time.

My point is, the cannabis plant, in some form or another, was already well-known and accepted all over the world *long* before it became vilified. And of course, every culture had its own slang for the plant—as I mentioned earlier, in Nigeria, we call it "igbo." We also call it "gbana," "kush," "blau," "oja," "weed," and, of course, "marijuana."

And, generally speaking, it's the same all over the world. While every culture has its own slang for cannabis, it's also known as "marijuana."

But *why?* The scientific name, "cannabis," I understand. But how did a term become so well-known, so universally accepted, that it shows up alongside "cannabis" in both popular culture and scientific journals all around the globe?

The answer can be traced right back here, to the United States. And it reveals an uncomfortable and ugly truth about our country's history.

If you comb through textbooks, newspaper reports and other media of the day, widespread use of the term "marijuana" didn't begin until the 1930s. In fact, up until about 1910, the plant and its extracts were known in the United States only as "cannabis."

Pharmaceutical-grade cannabis formulations were commonplace in Western medicine, as were any number of home remedies. It was a familiar treatment in Victorian times for relief from cramps, rheumatism, and even epilepsy.[1] Cannabis was found in a plethora of products manufactured by major pharmaceutical companies, with names you'll probably recognize: Squibb (now

---

1   "Historical Timeline: History of Marijuana as Medicine—2900 BC to Present," Britannica ProCon.org, last updated June 16, 2021, https://medical marijuana.procon.org/historical-timeline/.

Bristol-Myers Squibb). Eli Lilly. Upjohn. Parke-Davis. Abbott Laboratories.

Which raises another question: How did we get here? How do we now find ourselves fighting to legalize and legitimize a plant that has such vast medicinal potential; a plant whose extracts were once an integral part of legal medications, and whose fibers played an important part of manufacturing? A plant that has played a vital role in cultures, economies, and the growth of nations all around the world?

How do we find ourselves trying to undo almost a century's worth of damage and debasement?

The answers are tightly intertwined. And, like most bad decisions, the roots to our nation's disastrous drug policies can be found wrapped tightly around a cinder-block foundation of fear.

It's a fear that was twisted and manipulated by White men of means and power who sought only to further their political careers and personal fortunes, no matter the cost. Men with a racist agenda who had a total disregard for the truth and a complete disdain for people who didn't look, think or act like them.

And it's a fear that's still being twisted today; still being used to manipulate the masses and amass wealth for the already wealthy.

* * *

By most accounts, the term "marijuana" started to show up in the United States in the first quarter of the 1900s. Researchers point to a wave of immigration by Mexicans fleeing the decade-long Mexican Revolution. The logic goes that some of the immigrants used the word "marijuana" to describe the leaves and buds of the cannabis plants they rolled up and smoked.

In *Cannabis: The Illegalization of Weed in America*,[2] Philadelphia author/illustrator Box Brown posits that the origins of the word "marijuana" can be found in slang used to keep Mexican authorities in the dark. Catholic officials there took a dim view of the plant, and the country declared cannabis illegal in 1920.[3] To avoid detection, Brown writes, users would often refer to the plant by common girls' names, like "Rosa Maria," "Maria Rosa," or "Maria Juana."

Some version of this origin story—that the roots of the word "marijuana'" can be found in Mexican Spanish—has been generally accepted by scholars for decades. But Chris S. Duvall, professor and chair of geography and environmental studies at the University of New Mexico, turned that idea on its ear in 2019.

In *The African Roots of Marijuana*, Duvall points to evidence that the plant was in use on the African continent

---

2 Box Brown, *Cannabis: The Illegalization of Weed in America* (Philadelphia: First Second, 2019).

3 Isaac Campos, *Home Grown: Marijuana and the Origins of Mexico's War on Drugs* (Chapel Hill: University of North Carolina Press, 2012).

as early as the fourteenth century. And he reveals that a plural noun used in west Africa, "mariamba," meant "some cannabis to smoke."[4] That pronunciation and spelling of the word changed as the plant spread across the globe—and in 1846 turns up as "mariguana" in the textbook *Farmacopea Mexicana*. Later, the word was often spelled "marihuana," which is the term racist American lawmakers latched on to as they sought to vilify the plant *and* link it to Mexican immigrants.

But regardless of the true origin of the word, there were no widespread concerns about the consumption of "marijuana" in the early twentieth century. Some scholars say that's because cannabis use was already limited because of Mexico's ban. And other readily available drugs—such as heroin, cocaine, and opium—were causing very real problems across the United States.

In 1913, though, California prohibited the cultivation of cannabis as part of a wide-sweeping anti-narcotics bill aimed at reducing opiate abuse. The plant had been added merely as a "preventative" measure—there were no reported problems with abuse, and there were no federal regulations against the plant.

Then the Great Depression came along, and that, as they say, changed everything.

---

4   Chris Duvall, *The African Roots of Marijuana* (Durham, NC: Duke University Press, 2019).

As Americans came face-to-face with financial ruin, they became angry. How did they, the citizens of one of the most prosperous nations in the world, find themselves suddenly bankrupt, jobless, homeless? They cast about to blame someone—anyone—for their financial woes. And, as is often the case, immigrants became an easy target.

Racial discrimination, already bubbling close to the surface, suddenly boiled over: immigrants were to blame for the crumbling economy; immigrants had stolen jobs from the White working class; immigrants were destroying the American way of life.

Sound familiar?

Never mind that average Americans had stretched their budgets to the breaking point with new loans for cars and appliances, that there were few regulations in place to keep banks in check, and that economic growth was limited because "the richest one percent of Americans owned over a third of all American assets."[5] Never mind that the post–World War I US economy was already a house of cards waiting to crumble. Never mind that those who were complaining the loudest were themselves descended from immigrants.

Meanwhile, politicians with an eye on their careers and wallets did what most politicians do best: They used the xenophobic American public's fear and anger to their

---

5 "The Great Depression," U.S. History Pre-Columbian to the New Millennium, accessed November 5, 2019, http://www.ushistory.org/us/48 .asp.

political advantage. Soon, they adopted the word "mari-juana"—often spelling it with an "h" instead of a "j" to draw attention to its foreign sound (a practice that US government agencies persist in today). They railed against the plant from campaign stump to legislative branch, all the while declaring cannabis a foreign-born evil; a weed brought here by Mexican and Black immigrants—the same people who, the logic went, were also here to take away American jobs.

It made no difference that, during this same time period, cannabis was being used as an effective com-ponent in a wide array of existing, legal medications. It made no difference that they were lumping inert indus-trial hemp plants in with cannabis. It made no difference that there was *no evidence* that it was causing problems of any kind. Instead, the politicians called it "marijuana" to hoodwink the masses—and argued that it was a devilish substance; a foreign-born evil; a menace that would ruin minds and bodies and homes.

Ironic, then, that this name game would lead to a war on drugs that did exactly that.

* * *

In 1930, when Harry Anslinger was named the first direc-tor of the Federal Bureau of Narcotics—after a stint as a prohibition agent—he sealed the plant's fate. A savvy pol-itician, Anslinger knew he needed to drum up support for his newfound position. As Johann Hari writes in *Chasing the Scream: The First and Last Days of the War on Drugs,* "From the moment he took charge of the bureau, Harry was aware of the weakness of his new position. A war on narcotics alone—cocaine and heroin, outlawed in 1914—wasn't enough. They were used only by a tiny minority, and you couldn't keep an entire department alive on such small crumbs. He needed more."[6]

Anslinger was also a dyed-in-the-wool racist, with views so extreme it made his peers uncomfortable. In an interview with News Beat,[7] Hari says, "It's important to understand: [Anslinger] was regarded as a crazy racist in the 1920s. . . . He used the 'N' word so often in official government memos that his own senator said that he should have to resign. . . . The other group that he really hated were people with addiction problems—addicts."

Yet Anslinger was allowed to persist—and knew he could manipulate White America's fears to achieve his political agenda. He was full of outrageous, vile statements, like "Reefer makes darkies think they're as good as White men."[8] "Marihuana leads to pacifism and communist

6   Johann Hari, *Chasing the Scream: The First and Last Days of the War on Drugs* (New York: Bloomsbury USA, 2015), 18.

7   "Racism, Weed & Jazz: The True Origins of the War on Drugs," News Beat, August 25, 2017, https://usnewsbeat.medium.com/racism-weed-jazz-the-true-origins-of-the-war-on-drugs-8e6fd4ef813.

8   Tikkanen, Amy. "Why Is Marijuana Illegal in the U.S.?" Encyclopedia Britannica, Accessed 12 November 2021, https://www.britannica.com/story/why-is-marijuana-illegal-in-the-us.

brainwashing." "Marijuana causes White women to seek sexual relations with Negroes, entertainers, and any others."

In testimony before Congress, he said that "Marijuana is the most violence-causing drug in the history of mankind. . . . Most marijuana smokers are Negroes, Hispanics, Filipinos, and entertainers. Their satanic music, jazz and swing, result from marijuana usage."

Anslinger's fearmongering, racist crusade worked the public into a frenzy, even as he spoke out of both sides of his mouth. In a January 1939 edition of *The Union Signal*, described as a "journal of social welfare," Anslinger wrote, "The abuse of marijuana can be stamped out through preventative educational work. This can be done without sensationalism."

Meanwhile, newsreels, newspapers, and magazines ran stories—fed to them by Anslinger himself—that breathlessly proclaimed "marijuana" was being sold to schoolchildren from roadside taco and lemonade stands, that it drove users "loco," and that it was responsible for any number of atrocities from rape to murder to the "mingling of races." And state law enforcement authorities were ramping up arrests under "narcotic drug laws."

Police reports were inflated, and cases sensationalized—like when a Florida man killed his family with an axe in 1933. Police told the media that Victor Licata's "marijuana addiction" caused him to go on the killing spree. Not long after, they backpedaled on the claim—but not by much. Many years later it was disclosed that Licata had long suffered from mental illness, that there was no evidence of a cannabis connection, and that the Tampa police had tried to institutionalize him a year earlier.

Never let the facts get in the way of a good story, right?

* * *

In the United States, attempts to restrict and regulate cannabis sales began appearing in some states in the early 1900s. Most states simply required that any formulations containing cannabis list it as an ingredient. Others required a prescription for its use. In California, as I mentioned earlier, possession was quietly deemed a misdemeanor in 1913, as part of legislation dubbed the Poison Act. The next year, in what might be the first-ever cannabis raid, an inspector for the State Board of Pharmacy confiscated what was dubbed a "wagonload" of Indian hemp from two "dream gardens" in downtown Los Angeles.[9]

The nascent seeds of the drug war had been sown—and law enforcement officials didn't waste any time harvesting a growing crop of arrests.

---

9   Elyssa Dudley, "The nation's first marijuana raid likely happened in Los Angeles," Off-Ramp, September 19, 2014, https://archive.kpcc.org/programs /offramp/2014/09/19/39399/the-nation-s-first-marijuana-raid-likely -happened/.

In 1930, the federal Uniform Crime Reporting (UCR) Program began disseminating crime statistics for the United States and its territories. Making sense of early drug-related arrests isn't an easy task, however, in part because methods for accurately recording arrest rates were still being tested and refined. Those "Uniform Crime Reports" weren't especially uniform, because the number of agencies that sent reports to the Feds often changed with each passing year—sometimes increasing, sometimes dropping off. In fact, the reports themselves contain a disclaimer: "In publishing the data sent in by chiefs of police in different cities the United States Bureau of Investigation does not vouch for its accuracy."

But one thing seems clear: Arrests for cannabis, and drugs in general, were climbing. And while the UCRs don't give us the entire story, they do give us a pretty clear picture of what was going on.

The 1932 Uniform Crime Report[10] cites data received "from 1,578 cities in the United States . . . representing a population of 53,212,230."[11] The report also cites data from "82 percent of the cities over 10,000 in population."

The report then breaks the numbers down through a series of annotated tables listing data including offense

---

10 United States Department of Justice Federal Bureau of Investigation, Uniform Crime Reports [United States], 1930–1959, Inter-university Consortium for Political and Social Research, June 19, 2003, https://doi .org/10.3886/ICPSR03666.v1.

11 New York City, Atlanta, and a handful of smaller cities did not participate.

charged, yearly totals, daily averages, percentage of arrests by gender, age group, month, population size, and so on.

And from February 1 through December 31, 1932, a total of 2,648 people were charged under "narcotic drug laws."

By 1933—the year authorities blamed "marijuana addiction" for the Florida axe murders—the reporting area had increased by eighty cities; the population represented had jumped from 53,212,230 to 62,357,262, and the number of arrests under "narcotic drug laws" had grown to 3,370. Interestingly, the reports this year also start to include a table that breaks arrests down by race: White, Black, and "all others."

Even more interesting—given the spike in the number of arrests of Blacks that would come in about a quarter-century's time—is that the total number of Whites arrested in the United States on drug charges in 1933 far outweighs arrests of other races: 2,251 Whites vs. 362 Blacks and 757 "others." In fact, the report goes so far as to state, "Negroes constituted a comparatively small proportion of those charged with forgery and counterfeiting, embezzlement and fraud, offenses against the family, driving while intoxicated, *and violation of narcotic drug laws.*"

It's a similar story in 1934 and 1935. In 1936, the reports further break down the races to include "White, Negro, Chinese, Japanese, Mexican, and All Others"— but Whites still make up the majority of the growing number of narcotics arrests. However, in the years that follow, the number of Blacks and Mexicans charged with drug offenses steadily increases.

Meanwhile, Anslinger was slinging his anti-cannabis rhetoric left and right. In 1937, he penned a deceitful, inflammatory diatribe called "Marijuana: Assassin of Youth." It was filled with pithy, unsubstantiated passages like this:

"It would be well for law-enforcement officers everywhere to search for marijuana behind cases of criminal and sex assault. During the last year a young male addict was hanged in Baltimore for criminal assault on a ten-year-old girl. His defense was that he was temporarily insane from smoking marijuana. In Alamosa, Colo., a degenerate brutally attacked a young girl while under the influence of the drug. In Chicago, two marijuana smoking boys murdered a policeman."

Later that year, with support at a fever pitch, Anslinger was able to push through the Marihuana Tax Act. It essentially acted as a new Prohibition by imposing a $1 tariff and requiring anyone who sold or grew the plant to get a tax stamp. The stamps weren't issued, though—and you could get one only by incriminating yourself in the first place. The act didn't criminalize possession or use of cannabis per se, but imposed hefty penalties—like a fine of up to $2,000 and five years in prison—if you didn't pay the tax.

In 1939, skeptical New York Mayor Fiorello La Guardia, an opponent of the tax act, commissioned a study on the effects of cannabis by the New York Academy of Medicine.[12] Five years later, the group of scientists and doctors released a report that refuted every insane claim made by Anslinger. But Anslinger, furious, condemned it as unscientific and shut down further research.

He then went on a crusade to obliterate opposing information. In the face of all logic, he prosecuted doctors who were legally and successfully treating and managing real addicts—folks with a physical dependence on drugs like heroin and opium.[13] Anslinger had them discredited, stripped of their licenses, and effectively silenced. He also locked up musicians and actors, gaining plenty of airtime in the process.

Among his high-profile arrests were drummer Gene Krupa and actor Robert Mitchum. He mercilessly pursued Billie Holiday, right up to her deathbed. And with each year, each arrest of an "immoral" menace, he was able to write and rewrite the antidrug dialogue. It morphed as necessary, and soon he'd gone from stoking the fears of paranoid White parents to fanning the flames of anti-communism into a frenzy. He even brought his war to the UN, and before long had almost the entire world bending the knee on drug policy.

---

12 "Marijuana Regulation: The LaGuardia Report at 70 (Item of the Month)," History of Medicine and Public Health, New York Academy of Medicine, April 24, 2014, https://nyamcenterforhistory.org/2014/04/25 /marijuana-regulation-the-laguardia-report-at-70/.

13 Johann Hari, *Chasing the Scream: The First and Last Days of the War on Drugs* (New York: Bloomsbury USA, 2015), 34.

Anslinger finally retired in 1962, during the Kennedy administration, but he'd set the stage for every administration that followed. He was the nearly unbeatable opening act for the deadly dog and pony show that has gripped the nation every decade since.

And under his watch, the number of Blacks arrested on narcotics charges started to outpace Whites. According to the crime reports, that happened for the first time in 1950, with 3,018 Blacks arrested on narcotics charges vs. 2,563 Whites.

Then, in 1951, Congress passed the Boggs Act, which established mandatory minimum sentences for drug offenders—and the number of narcotics arrests leapt higher than ever: more than 13,000 total arrests, with 6,697 Blacks arrested versus 5,873 Whites. The UCR offers no explanation for the sudden spike—but it certainly seems to be tied to the Boggs Act.

By 1952, new data collection methods were used to populate the reports. Prior to this, police departments had been using only fingerprint data to record information on age, sex, and race—and not every arrest results in the recording of fingerprints. But now the reports would include *everyone* arrested in relation to a crime—regardless of whether they were fingerprinted. Yet in this first year using new data, the total number of narcotics-related arrests inexplicably falls to 3,103—and Whites arrested on narcotics charges outnumber Blacks 1,635 to 1,447, or by a total of 188 arrests.

Throughout the rest of the 1950s, however, narcotics-related arrests of Blacks outpace those of Whites; sometimes by more than double the numbers.

Then the tables turn. During the tumultuous 1960s, narcotics arrest rates steadily climb, and Whites are arrested at a *much* higher rate than Blacks on drug charges. In 1967, for instance, 57,146 Whites are arrested on drug charges. That same year, less than half that number—(22,848) of Blacks are arrested. In 1968, those numbers climb to 105,886 and 29,608, respectively.

A deeper look at the data soon reveals a probable cause: Most of those arrests were White youth under the age of eighteen. At the time, the baby boomer generation was protesting the Vietnam War. The Civil Rights Movement was in full swing. There were riots in the streets. Authorities were cracking down on cannabis (and other drugs) to find a way to gain some semblance of control.

President Lyndon B. Johnson launched a "War on Crime" in 1965, and for the first time, local police agencies were given access to military-grade equipment including rifles, gas masks, bulletproof vests, helicopters—even tanks. Then in 1968, he declared war again—this time "on the pushers of drugs and peddlers of LSD," seeking to hire two hundred more federal narcotics agents.[14]

In 1970, the ban on cannabis was included in the Controlled Substances Act. And in 1971, President

---

14 "LBJ Declares War on Pushers of Drugs and Peddlers of LSD," *Maderna Tribune*, February 8, 1968; https://cdnc.ucr.edu/?a=d&d=MT1968 0208.2.65&e=-------en--20--1--txt-txIN--------1.

Richard Nixon, eager to be seen as tough on crime (ironic in itself), officially declared the start of the war on drugs. When a government commission he'd formed to study cannabis instead called for decriminalizing its possession and distribution in 1972, he not only ignored their findings, he also tried to pressure the head of the commission—former Pennsylvania Governor Raymond Shafer—to reject the findings altogether![15]

In fact, in a 1994 interview, Watergate coconspirator John Ehrlichman, who was Nixon's counsel and assistant to the president for domestic affairs, told *Harper's Magazine* writer Dan Baum, "You want to know what this [war on drugs] was really all about? The Nixon campaign in 1968, and the Nixon White House after that, had two enemies: the antiwar left and Black people. You understand what I'm saying? We knew we couldn't make it illegal to be either against the war or Black, but by getting the public to associate the hippies with marijuana and Blacks with heroin, and then criminalizing both heavily, we could disrupt those communities. We could arrest their leaders, raid their homes, break up their meetings, and vilify them night after night on the evening

---

15 "Nixon Commission Report Advising Decriminalization of Marijuana Celebrates 30th Anniversary," NORML, March 21, 2002, https://norml .org/news/2002/03/21/nixon-commission-report-advising-decriminalization -of-marijuana-celebrates-30th-anniversary/

news. Did we know we were lying about the drugs? Of course we did."[16]

An admission of guilt, straight from the mouth of one of the leading horses of the day . . . and yet the war on drugs drags on. Surprised? Sadly, neither am I.

A Center for American Progress article estimates that in the four decades since the Nixon administration's madness, the drug war has cost America *$1 trillion*.[17] That same article states that *six times* more Americans have been arrested for possession than for dealing, and that the number of those arrests have tripled since 1980. In 2015, those arrest numbers hit 1.3 million, and they continue to grow—as does the racial gap. A 2020 ACLU study found that in some states, Blacks are nearly *10 times more likely* to be arrested than Whites on cannabis-related charges.[18]

The trail of facts and figures allows us to easily track how—and when—the cannabis story changed. It shows us who the major players were. It paints a clear picture of widespread public manipulation achieved through a careful campaign of disinformation. (Again, sound familiar?)

---

16 Dan Baum, "Legalize It All," Harper's Magazine, April 2016, https://harpers.org/archive/2016/04/legalize-it-all/.

17 Betsy Pearl, "Ending the War on Drugs: By the Numbers," Center for American Progress, June 27, 2018, https://www.americanprogress.org/issues/criminal-justice/reports/2018/06/27/452819/ending-war-drugs-numbers/.

18 "A Tale of Two Countries: Racially Targeted Arrests in the Era of Marijuana Reform," ACLU research report, 2020, https://www.aclu.org/report/tale-two-countries-racially-targeted-arrests-era-marijuana-reform.

The data strips away the veneer of *politispeak* to illustrate a solid core of racial injustice. And it precisely delineates the field in which the seeds of the drug war were sown, grown, and continue to be harvested.

When one looks back through history, one sees that these themes of inequality, of injustice, repeat themselves. Almost a quarter of the way into the twenty-first century, we're still trying to convince people that Black Lives Matter. We're still fighting for the rights of the LGBTQ community. We're still trying to prove that cannabis is a medicine, not a devil weed.

And I've barely started talking about the racial disparity that exists among those who were arrested because of the drug war, or the impact it's had on people's lives; on medicine; and on society as a whole.

In fact, I've only just scratched the surface.

CHAPTER 11

Racism and the War on Drugs: A Bitter Harvest Reaped

"Black people are 3.7 times more likely to be arrested for marijuana possession than their White peers even though they use marijuana at similar rates. If we truly want to be a fair and just nation we need to correct for this disparate treatment of enforcement practices."
—New Jersey Sen. Cory Booker, in a Feb. 28, 2019, tweet

In 2010, Bernard Noble was back in New Orleans—his childhood home—visiting family. He planned to take some time off; see his parents; and buy "hot sausage and French bread" for his restaurant in St. Louis.

That's when his life turned upside down.

Bernard, a father of seven, was on his way to his dad's electronics shop in a low-income neighborhood. He'd dropped his car off earlier to have TV monitors installed so his children could watch videos.

Suddenly, "five cars of police swung the corner," he told the Huffington Post.[1] He was with two other men, and one of them, scared, tossed away a small baggie of weed.

"The officers stopped us about ten feet from where he threw it, and the officers after searching found it. They gave no reason for the stop then, under oath they said that my reaction to them pulling up seemed suspicious," he said.

Bernard, who was riding a bike, says he moved only to avoid the police cars. He had no reason to worry—he hadn't been carrying the pot, after all, and didn't have any drugs on him. But police threw all three of them up against the cars. In a podcast on Drugpolicy.org, Bernard says he verbally challenged the cops, saying "I don't know what you're talking about" when he was questioned. That's when one of them said, "I'm gonna make sure your Black ass gets charged."

The other two men were released, but Bernard was arrested and charged with possession. The police report stated that officers found the pot—the equivalent of about two joints' worth—in one of his pockets.

From there, things turned from bad to worse. In 2011, Bernard was sentenced to thirteen years and three months of hard labor, with no possibility of parole.

---

1   "This Man Is Serving More Than 13 Years In Prison Over Two Joints' Worth Of Marijuana," HuffPost News, August 8, 2015, https://www.huffingtonpost .com/entry/bernard-noble-marijuana_us_55b6b838e4b0074ba5a5e160.

At this point, I hope you're scratching your head, wondering, "Why would he receive such a harsh sentence for such a miniscule amount of cannabis?"

If you are, you're not alone. Not one, but *two* trial judges who heard the case believed the thirteen-year sentence too harsh and tried to reduce it to five. But Orleans Parish District Attorney Leon Cannizzaro kept pushing back, pursuing the case right up to the Louisiana Supreme Court, where he finally won.

I ask you, does that seem like a logical use of resources? Why was so much time, money, and effort spent to jail a nonviolent offender for thirteen years over roughly two joints' worth of pot? The FBI's Uniform Crime Reports show that when Bernard was arrested, charged, and convicted, New Orleans had one of the highest murder rates in the country. And the city had a backlog of 830 untested rape evidence kits at the New Orleans Police Department—some dating back to the 1980s and 1990s, according to EndTheBacklog.org/louisiana.

So why wasn't the justice system focusing on more serious issues instead? There are four answers.

The first lies in the state's draconian drug laws,[2] which Bernard had run afoul of in the past. He had seven prior convictions, all for small amounts of drugs. Three of them, however, were felonies. Prosecutors

---

2   In 2015, the state reduced penalties for those caught with a small amount of marijuana, but it's still not enough.

used two of the felonies—one from 1991, another from 2003—to sentence him under Louisiana's "habitual offender" law. No matter that he'd never been convicted for a violent offense, no matter that the drugs were for personal use.

The second is the justice system's tendency to aim for the "low-hanging fruit." What's easier, pouring resources into cracking murder, corruption, and fraud cases, or boosting arrest and conviction numbers (and getting federal kickbacks) by going after people who don't have the financial wherewithal to mount a proper defense?

The third is politics. In a March 2016 episode of the documentary series *Weediquette*[3] focusing on Bernard's case, former New Orleans assistant district attorney Graham Bosworth says, "Ensuring that marijuana is a felony for multiple offenses, and ensuring that they can then multiple-bill,[4] means someone who is found with two joints can go to jail for thirteen years, twenty years . . . arguably and potentially the rest of their life."

The host, Krishna Andavolu, then asks, "Why is he so aggressive and so intent on maximizing prison time for people?"

Bosworth's reply: "I mean, he's a politician. He's running as the DA. . . . So, for political reasons, I'm sure,

---

3 Weediquette, "The War on Weed," Hulu video, 44:00, March 15, 2016, https://www.hulu.com/watch/5b6c9a47-49ad-4093-b93c-a49bc489b7bc.

4 A practice used to increase the length of prison sentences for habitual offenders.

he wanted to say, 'Look, I'm putting people in jail for as long as possible,' because obviously, that's something you're going to run for re-election on. And that's part of your platform as a candidate."

Bosworth then goes on to put the final nail in the coffin: "Leon Cannizzaro, the district attorney in New Orleans, has come out and said, 'Having marijuana illegal makes my job easier because marijuana's an easy arrest.' "

The fourth answer (though maybe it should be the first), of course, is racism—and Bosworth finishes the *Weediquette* interview by saying, "As an attorney who both prosecuted marijuana cases and defends marijuana cases, the vast majority of the clients and/or defendants I was dealing with were African American."

Bernard was freed on parole in 2018 when the Orleans Parish District Attorney's Office finally agreed to reduce his sentence. He spent seven years behind bars. His children lost seven years with their father. He lost seven years of his life. All because he's Black and became another victim in the misguided war on cannabis.

Bernard Noble's story is frighteningly common. All across the country, hundreds of thousands of people have been—and are being—locked up over cannabis. Some of them are facing ridiculously long sentences. And the majority are Black or Brown.

Here in Philadelphia, where I live, African Americans represent about 44 percent of the population. Yet according to local news outlet *Billy Penn*, citing the Pennsylvania

Uniform Crime Reporting System,[5] between 2015 and 2018, African Americans made up 76 percent of all arrests for cannabis possession in the city.

The kicker: in 2014, then–Philly mayor Michael Nutter signed an ordinance stating that anyone caught with less than an ounce of cannabis could get a $25 ticket instead of jail.

Yet the arrests continue.

The numbers are even more skewed at the federal level. A 2017 story from *U.S. News & World Report*,[6] citing data from the U.S. Sentencing Commission, showed that 77 percent of federal cannabis sentences were handed down to Hispanics in 2016—even though Hispanics represent "less than 20 percent of the U.S. population."

And in 2020, an American Civil Liberties Union analysis of arrest rates concluded that Black people are 3.64 times more likely than White people to be arrested for cannabis possession—even though they use cannabis at comparable rates. The authors wrote, "In every single state, Black people were more likely to be arrested for marijuana possession, and in some states, Black people

5   Max Marin, "Philly Police Still Arrest Way More Black People for Pot than Anyone Else," *Billy Penn*, January 8, 2019, https://billypenn.com /2019/01/08/black-people-in-philly-are-still-arrested-disproportionately -for-buying-marijuana/.
6   Steven Nelson, "Latinos Got 77 Percent of Federal Pot Sentences Last Year," *U.S. News & World Report*, March 15, 2017, https://www.usnews.com/news /articles/2017-03-15/latinos-got-77-percent-of-federal-pot-sentences-last -year.

were up to six, eight, or almost ten times more likely to be arrested. In 31 states, racial disparities were actually larger in 2018 than they were in 2010."[7]

So why the disparity? Why are people still getting locked up for simple cannabis possession? And why are so many of them Black and Brown?

Because our legal system relies on an eight-decade-old, racist, *sadistic,* misguided approach to law enforcement. Because our law enforcement agencies are still following in the footsteps of Harry Anslinger. Because the war on drugs is paying for bonuses, massive amounts of overtime, and equipment that, in some cases, rivals that of the military. Because it's easy to drum up support by stoking public fears; because it's easy to get convictions when you target disenfranchised people in poor neighborhoods who can't afford the best lawyers to fight back. (When was the last time you heard of police canvassing rich, White neighborhoods in their search for drug users?)

Because politics, not justice, are setting arrest and sentencing guidelines.

And to add insult to injury, scores of law enforcement officers across the nation—many of them on federally funded drug task forces—have been caught up in scandals involving the sale of the illegal drugs they seized!

---

7   "A Tale of Two Countries: Racially Targeted Arrests in the Era of Marijuana Reform," ACLU Research Report, American Civil Liberties Union, 2020.

The following statistics, borrowed from the Center for American Progress[8] and the ACLU,[9] represent part of the harvest from the crop of racial disparity planted by Harry Anslinger and carefully nurtured by every US president since:

- Blacks are four times more likely to be arrested on cannabis charges than Whites, even though both use cannabis almost equally.
- Blacks make up almost 30 percent of all drug-related arrests but make up just 12.5 percent of substance users.
- Almost 80 percent of people serving time for a federal drug offense are Black or Latino.
- In state prisons, people of color make up 60 percent of those serving time for drug charges.

And here's what that harvest has cost the United States since Nixon's 1971 declaration of war: about $1 trillion.

To put that in perspective, that's a one, followed by twelve zeros. A million million. According to The Calculator Site,[10] if you stacked $1 trillion in $100 dollar bills it would reach 631 miles into the sky.

---

8   Betsy Pearl, "Ending the War on Drugs: By the Numbers," Center for American Progress, June 27, 2018, https://www.americanprogress.org/issues /criminal-justice/reports/2018/06/27/452819/ending-war-drugs-numbers/.
9   "The War on Marijuana in Black and White," ACLU Research Report, American Civil Liberties Union, 2013.
10   "How Much Is a TRILLION?" The Calculator Site, last modified February 15, 2021, https://www.thecalculatorsite.com/articles/finance/how-much-is -a-trillion.php.

Think—*think*—of the good that could have been done with that money!

But here's something that hardly ever gets mentioned when we talk about the cost of the drug war; about the war on cannabis: the human cost.

How many families have been ripped apart? How many fathers and mothers torn from their children? How many kids have grown up with gang members as role models, instead of parents?

The truth is, we'll probably never know.

It's staggering . . . sickening, when you think about it.

What's more, a drug conviction—even a misdemeanor—can follow a person for life. It can lead to being denied a job, a loan, a place to live, the right to vote. It can lead to the loss of driving privileges, financial aid, even a professional license—a convicted doctor or lawyer might never practice again.

Where is the logic in locking up people—in some cases, for decades—simply for possession of cannabis?

And furthermore, as a nation, how are we still okay with allowing life-shattering drug convictions on one hand, and encouraging record-breaking cannabis profits on the other? It is inconceivable to me that a state would even have a program without first setting the record straight. That has been one of the biggest failures so far.

In 2020 alone, the regulated cannabis industry in the United States, as a whole, raked in more than $17.5 billion in cannabis sales! People are making billions; taxes are being collected hand over fist at the state and federal level; and cannabis has been declared legal, in some form or other, in at least thirty-seven states as of this writing.

And yet the arrests continue.

We have a responsibility here to set the record straight. That means freeing everyone who is in jail as a result of a nonviolent cannabis-related charge, wiping their records clean, and giving them a chance at life in whatever form it can be salvaged.

And we have a responsibility to do right by the untold number of children who grew up without one parent, or both, because of the war on drugs. That means wiping clean the records of anyone who has *ever* had a nonviolent cannabis-related conviction. It means helping to rebuild the communities the war has torn apart. And it means telling the public the whole, ugly truth about the war on drugs.

There's certainly hope: As of publication, more than twenty states have already passed reforms linked to cannabis-related convictions, and eleven of those include automatic expungement—meaning victims won't need to petition to have their records cleared. And in September 2021, the Marijuana Opportunity, Reinvestment and Expungement (MORE) Act was cleared by the House Judiciary Committee—meaning it can now be scheduled for a vote by the full House. Will it pass the Senate and White House? Only time will tell—but I believe there is a momentum in place now that cannot be stopped.

We cannot bring back the people who have died. We cannot patch up the broken homes, the fractured families, or the shattered lives. The war on drugs has stained our past, is staining our present, and will stain our future if we stand by and do nothing. It's time to roll up our sleeves and get to work.

The war on drugs has to stop, and the rebuilding must begin.

CHAPTER 12

If It Quacks Like a Duck, Don't Call It a Goose

It's time to talk about the (white) elephant in the room: reforming this country's regressive, oppressive, asinine cannabis laws and policies.

While President Biden's 2022 pardon of federal convictions for simple marijuana possession offenses is a promising start, I'm talking about real reform, not just lip service: Legalization on a federal level. Sweeping expungement of records at both the state and federal levels. Economic growth for the disenfranchised Black and Brown communities that have been primarily affected by the war on drugs.

And by economic growth, I mean access to jobs—real jobs—that are in the cannabis industry. I mean access to training for those jobs.

Because right now, in my home state of Pennsylvania, and many other states, a person with a cannabis-related conviction cannot work in the medical cannabis space. In fact, that person can't even *volunteer* in the medical cannabis space.

In Pennsylvania, it's spelled out in a provision of Act 16 that refers to a conviction for "any criminal offense related to the sale or possession of illegal drugs, narcotics or controlled substances."

But here's the thing that *really* blows my mind: That same provision doesn't prohibit me from hiring people with convictions for white-collar crimes like fraud, bribery, embezzlement, tax evasion, and racketeering. And guess who's convicted in the majority of those crimes?

White males.[1]

So let me get this straight: A person of color who was busted on a drug-related charge when he was nineteen, and convicted, even if he never did jail time—even if, in the face of all of that, he went on to become a successful, honest, hardworking adult—is considered a threat to the industry, a threat to the medical cannabis program; but on the flip side, a White male, who as an adult, was busted for corporate embezzlement, or tax evasion, or even *arson*, is not?

How does that even make sense?

It doesn't, unless you see it for what it really is: a continuation of the racist policies designed to further repress

---

1   "The Measurement of White-Collar Crime Using Uniform Crime Reporting (UCR) Data," U.S. Department of Justice Office of Justice Programs, 2000.

the minorities who have already been unfairly affected by the war on drugs. The same people who are *still* being repressed by the war on drugs.

Like the mother who is working multiple jobs to support her family but doesn't have insurance and cannot afford medicine to relieve her chronic pain, or her anxiety, or her insomnia. Who *has* to work multiple jobs because the father of her children is locked up, because he got caught with a joint.

If she opts to follow the rules, to go the legal route and submit her information to the state to get her medical cannabis card, she is then in danger of losing her federal housing—because the Fed's zero tolerance laws that apply to her housing don't make a distinction between state-legal medical cannabis and illegal drugs. The Federal Controlled Substances Act makes any type of marijuana use illegal, and Title 42 of the United States Code of Federal Regulations states that the landlord can "terminate the tenancy or assistance for any household with a member who the public housing agency or owner determines is illegally using a controlled substance."

Now, I'm not advocating that people break the law. But let's take a look at reality: We are all medicating something. And she knows where she can get medicine that safely helps her: her street connection.

She can go to him in confidence and get affordable— albeit illegal—medical cannabis that's sold on the black market. She knows her connect, her "street doc," will be able to say, "Oh, you have back pain? This strain will work for you. Anxiety? Then you want this strain. Can't sleep? That strain will work for you."

And she knows that she can go visit him under the radar, with no records kept. And she feels more secure that way; she trusts him.

Now, if that street doc gets busted, then she's forced to go to someone else; someone who doesn't have the strain she needs, but does have black-market opioids. Maybe it's a combination of other pharmaceuticals like opioids, anti-depressants, and muscle relaxants. And her pain is such that she's desperate for relief—and she needs to work—so now she's taking a far more dangerous (and addictive) product illegally.

And she soon joins the ranks of the millions of Americans who've become hooked on painkillers, regardless of how they were obtained.

That mother, and those like her, are the kind of people we're trying to reach, and help. But we *can't get to them* because one, they're disenfranchised; two, they've been victimized; and three, they don't trust.

And why would they?

Why would they trust the same government that controls medical cannabis cards with one hand, and disproportionally arrests Blacks and Hispanics with the other?

Now, let's look at this differently. Let's say the laws were changed. And let's say that street doc who got busted becomes rehabilitated. He does his time. He pays his debt.

Imagine, now, that he becomes a legitimate representative, or a community liaison, for the state's medical cannabis program. He can go into the local barbershop and help people sign up for their medical cannabis cards. He can talk to the community in a language they understand.

Wouldn't that be a better way to get illicit drugs off the street? Wouldn't that be a better way to clean up our neighborhoods? Wouldn't that be a better way to empower those same people who have been ground under the heel of the war on drugs?

You're giving this guy a job, so he can feed his family. He's helping the mom with chronic back pain get a card, so she can keep her jobs and feed *her* family. And maybe now she can go to a clinic in her own neighborhood, run by people she knows and trusts, who also have good-paying jobs.

I wish that could happen. I wish I could hire those people, train them, and give them the tools to go back into the community and help clean it up, help bring people real relief. They are the best educators, the best candidates to bring about change. And they deserve a shot to rebuild their neighborhoods and their lives.

But again, we need reform first. And if we're going to set things right, that reform will include changes to the employment provision, too. Instead of an outright ban, I suggest that we require a reasonable number of years to have passed without a drug-related conviction before you can work in the medical cannabis space.

Because I cannot tell you how many smart, qualified people I've had to say "no" to because of a cannabis-related conviction. Each time, I think, *I'd hire this guy in an instant . . . but I can't.*

And my experience roughly mirrors the same statistics we talked about in the last chapter: For every *one* White male who's told me he has a cannabis-related conviction, I've had to turn away five or six African Americans! And these are people who have their lives together, people who got busted a long time ago and still have the conviction on their record—in some cases, more than fifteen or twenty years ago!

People who would be a serious asset to our industry.

And it's infuriating! It's flat-out wrong! It's ridiculous that a person who got busted with a joint twenty years ago is 1) still struggling to get that conviction cleared up and 2) can't work in this space!

It's easy to say, "Yeah, but they broke the law." Well, guess what? Someone who stole thousands, who cheated the government, who committed bribery or fraud, also broke the law. And they could cause *serious damage* in the medical cannabis space.

But they can get hired, and I might never know about those convictions because by law I don't have to ask. By law, I don't have to exclude them. But by law, I *do* have to exclude the people who could be a huge asset, the people whom this could help the most.

As I said in the last chapter, though, there is hope. And I applaud the people who are putting real hands and feet behind legislation that promises real criminal justice reform, real reform of the laws surrounding cannabis. And because of them—because of people like Rep. Jordan A. Harris, from Philadelphia County's 186th Legislative District—I am confident we will see that change soon.

Harris is a vocal critic of the current laws and is working hard to get legalization passed that supports record expungement.

"We're talking about people who cannot now get gainfully employed because they were smoking a substance that is not harmful to anyone," he said at a 2018 cannabis reform rally at the capitol in Harrisburg. "We're talking about an industry that we've now legalized for medical purposes, but those who were selling the same product five years ago, five months ago, are still being hampered by their criminal records. It is unconscionable that corporations and companies will now be able to make money off medical cannabis, but guys and women in my district are still being hindered by their criminal record for doing the same exact thing."

I couldn't agree more. And I am calling on voters who should open their eyes. Do not be bamboozled into supporting half-measures. These should not be concessions. On a federal and state level, legalization should come with record expungement. And our employment policies need to be changed.

Anything else is just an intentional handcuffing of the people who've already suffered the most; a continuation of the racism that was the cornerstone of Harry Anslinger's crusade; racism that then became the cornerstone of the war on drugs. Seeking real justice can come only from seeking change through the statutes of the law. And until the laws read differently, we should not expect different outcomes.

If it smells like a duck, quacks like a duck, and *looks* like a duck . . . don't come running to me calling it a goose.

CHAPTER 13

Closing Thoughts

The ancient Greek playwright Aeschylus said, "From a small seed a mighty trunk may grow."

And just as I have experienced personal growth since those early days at university, and even since starting this book, I have also seen growth, both across the country and across the world.

Around the time we received our approval to start the Ilera project in 2016, twenty-eight states allowed legal access to medical cannabis, and eight states allowed responsible adult use. A growing crop of lawmakers had taken up the mantle of change, and seeds of hope were being scattered across the country.

By the time I finished this book, in 2023, medical use was legal in thirty-eight states; responsible adult use was legal in twenty-three states; President Biden had announced federal pardons for those convicted of simple cannabis possession; and multiple bills seeking to decriminalize cannabis and, in some cases, bring some form of social equity for those most affected by the war on drugs, had been introduced by lawmakers at both the state and federal levels. Worldwide, more than forty countries allowed cannabis in some form, and more have been taking up the issue every day.

Meanwhile, our team at Zelira has already developed a number of cutting-edge cannabis-based treatments targeting specific conditions, including diabetes, insomnia, autism, chronic pain, oral care, neuropathy, and Parkinson's disease, and continue to do more.

It's a privilege to be standing here; it's a privilege to be a part of all this; it's a privilege to live in such interesting times; and it's a privilege to be at the forefront of a revolution in healthcare. It's almost like the breaking of a new day; like the dawn has lifted a sort of veil that's been covering this unique plant, and now we can begin to study it and look toward a future where cannabis is a part of our therapeutic repertoire.

The mighty trunk continues to widen, and I am grateful for the privilege to be among those tending to its growth. I believe that my work with medical cannabis is an opportunity to give life to the next generation of therapeutic agents that not only address very complex disease states, but also do so in a way that brings needed and accessible relief to patients. Because the reason we are doing all this, in case we forget, is the patients: patients who have been relegated—by the very legal system that sought to protect them—to using drugs that often have painful and serious side effects, not the least of which is addiction. In other words, patients who should have the right to use far safer cannabis-based medicines have too long been forced, by men of privilege, to use products that cause at least as many ills as they claim to treat.

Because despite all of our progress to date, there's still much work to be done. In the United States, and in many other places across the globe, cannabis is still very illegal. In some places, like my home country, you can't even talk about it without fear of societal or legal repercussions.

So to have the opportunity, the privilege, to live in a place where I get to be a leader by being part of one of the first licensed medical cannabis healthcare companies in Pennsylvania . . . and to be an African American man who gets to participate in addressing some of the societal and legal issues as an opinion leader; as a business leader; and as an industry leader—all of those have made me really, really think about the privilege I have to be alive at a time like this. I don't take that for granted, and I'm excited by the possibilities.

I feel like it is a privilege to be at the forefront of a new type of medicine, and to get to be a leader who can address the social injustices that have, for far too long, surrounded this plant. This plant is a wonder of nature and a miracle of God—not a substance to be banned, its users shunned and locked away.

I feel like it is a privilege to be able to try to set right some of the issues the generations before us got wrong in the war on drugs—a war that unjustly took so many parents, mostly Black and Brown, out of the home and destroyed so many lives. And I feel like if we get it right now, our children can grow up to a better future than their fathers and mothers were offered, have opportunities their fathers and mothers were denied, and become better fathers and mothers themselves.

I also feel like it is a privilege to have connected with Patrick O'Donnell, editor of this book. We met through a project that didn't pan out, but connected over our mutual passion for setting the record straight on cannabis. It's been a privilege to learn his story, and to discover the parallels and common denominators that have brought us closer as we've worked together.

It is a privilege to lead a team of highly motivated world-changers as we think through building, developing, commercializing, and validating cannabinoid-based medicine. In the last twenty-four months, we have achieved groundbreaking results in our clinical trials; we have taken creative regulatory initiatives to advance the understanding and the development of cannabinoid-based medicines; we have turned a non-net-revenue-generating biotech company into a revenue-generating biotech company; we have raised millions of dollars and deployed millions of dollars in clinical research, in product development, in technology development . . . all with the goal of advancing our position in this space.

President Barack Obama once said, "Change will not come if we wait for some other person or some other time. We are the ones we've been waiting for. We are the change that we seek." I hope this book inspires you to pick up the mantle of change; to become part of the change; to challenge the status quo and even your own thinking around cannabis; and to become an advocate for the restoration of rights that so long ago were unjustly stripped by self-serving politicians and bigots who sought personal glory and profit over the greater public good. We have the momentum; now is the time to carry it forward, toward progress, better medicines, and a brighter future.

We are at the tip of the spear.

Afterword
Common Denominators

by Patrick O'Donnell

"We are more alike, my friends, than we are unalike."
—Maya Angelou, "Human Family"

When I began working on this book with 'Dare seven years ago, it never occurred to me to look at the project in terms of our different skin tones or life experiences. We hit it off instantly, worked together seamlessly, and were on exactly the same wavelength most of the time.

Then, about a year into it, I was discussing the project with a friend over a few drinks. Our conversation turned to some of the statistics I'd uncovered during my research. He shook his head in astonishment at the arrest rate disparity between Blacks and Whites, then held up a hand and interrupted me. "Hold on," he said. "I've been meaning to ask: How does a relatively straitlaced White guy raised in rural Pennsylvania end up writing a book about pot with a Black Nigerian who lives in Philadelphia? How did you two connect? And how do you write in his voice, from his perspective?"

They were legitimate questions, and you might be asking them as well. Because on the surface, I suppose, it seems an unlikely pairing. But the more 'Dare and I got to know each other, the more we discovered parallels in our lives and worldviews. And I'm grateful to say that as we swapped stories about childhood, family traditions, and upbringing, we found that our differences only made our collaboration stronger. We found like minds with a shared passion for uncovering the truth, no matter how ugly. I felt (and still feel) very privileged to have the opportunity to work on this project.

'Dare and I met for the first time in 2017, when I was working at a former Bryn Mawr marketing and communications agency called Hollister Creative. He'd tasked our team with putting together a proposal for the newly formed Ilera Healthcare—and I was given the job of researching everything I could find out about this tenacious start-up and Pennsylvania's brand-new medical cannabis laws.

I was hooked from the start. The research into Ilera and its founders alone was fascinating. But the real gem, for me, was the very act of digging through the details of Pennsylvania's Medical Marijuana Act.

In the end, Ilera chose another, much larger vendor for its communications needs. But 'Dare had been impressed by our work, and came back with a new proposal: Write a book detailing his personal journey into the medical cannabis space. I jumped into the project eagerly—this was far more interesting than the dry, sales-oriented content I was writing for B2B websites.

But later that year, Hollister downsized, and I found myself with a choice: Try my luck getting a new job as I stared at the upside of fifty, or finally follow my passion and strike out on my own as a freelance writer and author.

It was, to say the least, a frightening choice for a single dad of two young boys, especially considering my life had already changed drastically over the previous five years. There'd been a difficult divorce, two job changes, and a number of personal challenges—including a battle to get one of my sons a diagnosis and treatment for autism and ADHD.

To add to my already full plate, just before I learned of my impending layoff, my dad began a series of hospitalizations. A very stubborn man, he'd long been ignoring nagging symptoms and familial appeals to see a doctor—and now he was dying of cancer.

So, I did what any sane, middle-aged, almost-broke man would do.

I decided to go for it.

Hollister's president, Kim Landry, kept me on as a steady freelancer while she worked to restructure the company, and 'Dare and I managed to pound out a few chapters while I worked to build up a client base and publish my first children's book.

To accommodate our busy lives, we devised a system: 'Dare would make recordings of his thoughts whenever his hectic (some might say insane) schedule allowed, then email them to me. I'd write them up, editing and adding research until they formed a cohesive narrative. We'd schedule calls as time allowed, filling in the gaps with occasional meetings where we'd share our thoughts over lunch.

But there were more challenges coming my way: My father died in January 2018—the first month I went solo. I found myself struggling to help my mom clean out and sell their seriously cluttered farm—an hour and a half away in the Poconos—while simultaneously trying to launch a new business and care for my sons.

And then, just a few months into the project with 'Dare, came the final blow: Kim told me Hollister would be absorbed by another company, and my position was no longer required. She graciously offered to let me keep a few of the clients with whom I'd been working—including 'Dare, who I'm grateful to say was eager to continue our collaboration. But I had lost my safety net, and with all the other stressors that had already piled up, I felt panic creeping in around the edges.

I briefly considered getting a full-time job doing just about anything *but* writing. But Dad wasn't the only stubborn one in the family, and I was determined that the only boss I'd ever answer to again would be myself. So I put my head down, dug my heels in, and slowly but steadily found my way forward. I took on some new clients, took on even more work with a satisfied existing client, and buried myself in the cannabis book.

And as our work progressed, 'Dare and I discovered more common denominators: Our thought process, for instance, is similar. That alone allowed me to "get in his head" as I was working on the chapters.

Then, as we hammered out "What Was the Progress Today?"—the chapter dealing with his father's illness—I was reminded of my own dad's struggle with a syndrome that's often called "preleukemia," and how family and friends had to push him to even seek a diagnosis when he became ill.

I found myself wondering, again and again, if cannabis could have helped him in any way—even if just to ease his pain or improve his appetite. It was a train of thought I'd quickly derailed when he was undergoing treatment, because I knew there was no way he would have considered it. Even though he was a lifelong Democrat, the foundation of his worldview was, after all, set in the brick and mortar laid by the likes of Harry Anslinger.

Later, when 'Dare told me about the first time he tried pot, I was brought back to the first time I tried it. Because despite an age difference of some twenty years, we had both been raised with the message of the drug war ringing in our ears—and we'd both bought into it hook, line, and sinker . . . until college.

But my first time, and the path I took from there, was profoundly different than 'Dare's.

Like 'Dare, I was a pretty straitlaced kid in high school. While others around me experimented with drugs and alcohol, I kept my head buried in books, band, the school newspaper, and (briefly) track. First of all, I was terrified of Mom and Dad—especially Dad. But I also genuinely feared drugs would permanently turn my brain to mush. Out of sheer rebelliousness, I once tried a few puffs of a joint at (of all places) a roller-skating rink. But the cannabis didn't have any effect other than to make me worry my parents would somehow find out. That worry was enough to make me "Just Say No" for another two years—because like 'Dare, I'd once gotten in big trouble over just a cigarette.

Then, as a freshman in college, I tried pot again—but this time was a vastly different experience. Like many college students, I was exploring my newfound freedom and pushing that exploration to the limits. On the afternoon in question, I was hanging out with my best friend—we'll call him Sean—after class. He procured a joint from somewhere and cranked up the Jimi Hendrix Experience album *Are You Experienced?* "Let's smoke this, dude. It'll change how you think about music," he said.

He was so, so right. I'd never listened to much Hendrix before then—the few songs I'd heard just hadn't resonated with me. But on that sunny autumn afternoon, it all came into focus. There was a speaker on either side of my head, and I remember, clear as a bell, the moment the music started to split and seemingly float between my ears.

"Whoa!" I said, and my friend nodded and smiled.

And so began a series of adventures—many good, some not so much—that reshaped my view of the war on drugs and cannabis in general.

Although I was mostly interested in its relaxing, music-enhancing effects back then, I soon found that for many people, pot wasn't just a recreational pastime. And suddenly, it seemed like almost everybody I knew or met was—or had been—a pot smoker.

First it was classmates and friends. Then it was professors, employers, and even members of my extended family! I felt like I'd gone down a rabbit hole of enlightenment about how the world worked . . . a journey that began with a single toke.

I also found that pot wasn't just for zoning out and getting "in tune" with music. One morning after a particularly raucous party, a buddy observed me suffering from a singularly nasty hangover.

"Hey, you should smoke some weed, dude. Cure that right away," he said as I rushed for the bathroom, one hand over my mouth and the other over my eyes to block the dazzling light.

I was skeptical, but soon found he was absolutely right. And so I was introduced not only to the concept of "wake and bake," but also to the notion that cannabis could be medicine. That led to my own research—both firsthand, and in the university library, where of course I found very little because of the federal regulations surrounding the plant.

The semesters passed, and despite our many misadventures, Sean and I were cautious and managed to avoid getting caught until one fateful spring afternoon. There were four or five of us hanging out in another friend's dorm room—let's call him Matt—when somebody produced a baggie of weed.

As was the usual practice, a window was opened, a fan set up, incense was lighted, and a damp towel rolled up and carefully placed to keep smoke from escaping under the door jamb. Soon we were passing around a bowl while Robert Plant wailed, *"In the evening . . . when the day is done . . ."*

Everything was "cool, dude, cool" . . . until suddenly, it wasn't. There was a sharp rapping on the door, and we all froze.

It was Matt's roommate. We'll call him Stewie—and Stewie was known for two things: his lack of discretion, and his habit of drawing out the word "man" like it was a ten-letter word.

"Hey, maaaaaaaan, lemme in," he yelled loudly, banging on the door again. "I know you guys are smokin' weed in there, maaaaaaaan! Lemme in!"

We panicked. This was late afternoon, and the floor's resident adviser would be roaming the halls. He had a reputation for busting students for the most minor of infractions—and he didn't like *our* crowd at all.

We stashed the bowl and the baggie. We waved the incense stick around the room to mask the smell, so it wouldn't waft into the hall when Matt opened the door. "Hold on, Stewie, we'll be there in a sec," Matt said.

"C'mon, maaaaaaaan, lemme in! I wanna get high!" Stewie protested loudly.

"Stewie, shut the hell up!" Matt hissed through the door. "You wanna get us busted? Gimme a minute."

Then came another, sharper knock, and a different voice: "Open the door *right now*, guys."

It was the resident adviser. And we all got that sinking feeling that comes when things have gone very, very wrong.

Thankfully, the RA wasn't the brightest bulb in the circuit. As soon as the door was unlocked, he burst in, but the only evidence remaining was the lingering smell of pot mixed with incense.

"OK, where is it?" he demanded.

"Where's what?" we asked innocently. "You know damn well what," he replied. He did a cursory search—opening drawers and wardrobes, looking under the two beds—but couldn't find anything. "You'll be hearing from the dean. I've got you guys now," he said self-righteously, spinning on his heel and marching out of the room.

Talk about a buzzkill. Our hearts sank. We returned to our own rooms and awaited our fate, certain the next knock would be the police.

That knock never came, but a few days later, we received a summons to the dean's office. Curiously, though, Sean and I were the only two names listed—even though there had been five of us in the room, not counting Stewie. I broke out the student handbook and started reading the section dealing with drugs and dorm-room busts. They hadn't actually caught us with anything, so I was hopeful. Maybe we could talk our way out of it.

The meeting with the dean didn't last very long. It turns out the resident adviser—who, like I said, wasn't exactly detective material—had screwed up just about everything to do with his "bust."

The handbook stated that he should have called campus police immediately. He hadn't. It also stated that he needed to get the IDs of everyone in the room. He hadn't. And to make matters even worse, he was able to identify only Sean and I by name—he had *no idea* who else had been in the room.

The dean tried his best to scare us into filling in the massive blanks. "I want the names of everyone else who was with you," he barked. Then he jabbed his finger at us. "You're all finished here, but maybe you can avoid jail."

It was like a scene from *Animal House*, with our very own inept, churlish Dean Wormer—only we didn't find anything funny about it. I wasn't sure about Sean, but I knew I couldn't count on any sympathy from the home front. If anything, my parents would take the dean's side—after all, this was the late 1980s. Ron and Nancy's "Just Say No" war was in full effect, and the Partnership for a Drug-Free America's "This is your brain on drugs" commercials were everywhere. And my dad, an ex-cop . . .

well, he alone was a force to be reckoned with. I was more afraid of him than I was of the police.

But, armed with the handbook, I knew we had a fighting chance. I recited the section that applied to the busts, pointing out that it was just the resident adviser's word against ours. He hadn't collected our IDs. He didn't know who was in the room with us. He hadn't found or even seen the "alleged pot." He hadn't called campus police. The only thing he had to go on was Stewie saying, "I know you're smoking weed!"; a vague, lingering skunky smell; and a bunch of guys with glassy eyes.

The dean, I think, knew he was beaten, but he blustered. He sputtered. He yelled, "Give me those damn names *right now*, or I'm having you two expelled!"

"And if you do that," I coolly bluffed right back, "my parents will have a lawyer here so fast your head will spin. Your RA didn't follow procedure. You have no evidence. You've got nothing on us. We were just sitting around listening to music and burning incense."

"You're a snake, O'Donnell! A snake!" he screamed, spittle flying from his mouth as his face turned redder than a rush-hour traffic light. He jumped up, pounded his fist on the desk, started to come around it toward us, then stopped midway, pointed to the door, and screamed "Get out! You'll hear from me soon!" As we left, he slammed the door shut so hard it knocked a picture off the wall behind his startled secretary. I'm pretty certain he wanted to *literally* kick us on the way out.

A few days later, despite the lack of evidence, we ended up getting a suspension that would end Sean's track career and force me to step down as the newspaper editor. And the next semester, Sean and I were informed we couldn't live on campus again.

I suppose we really could have fought it, but it was far better than going to jail or getting expelled, and the suspension was for misconduct—it never mentioned cannabis. I had to tell Mom a very edited version of the story. To say she wasn't happy is an understatement. But knowing Dad might very well boot me into the next century, she covered for me. Sean was in a similar boat, so we were just happy to take our lumps and move on.

Why am I sharing this story? Because today I know something I was wholly unaware of then: my friend and I had been on the receiving end of White privilege.

Sure, I had been able to talk our way out of it. Yes, the RA had badly bungled his bust. But I am *certain* that if our skin had been Black or Brown or any color other than White, things would have gone differently from the get-go.

Campus police would have been called immediately; then the borough police. And we'd not only have been kicked out of school, we'd also have been doing jail time and had our names and faces splashed across the local paper with a headline like, "Two nabbed in university pot sting." Because that was happening all around us—especially to people who looked more like 'Dare and less like Sean and me.

We just didn't have our eyes open enough to see it.

That incident was more than thirty years ago. I still keep in touch with Sean, and we sometimes have a laugh over our misadventures and close calls (yes, there were more). But most times, those laughs are strained. We both realize now how lucky we were; and how blissfully unaware we were back then of the drug war's widening ring of devastation.

Coincidentally, the day after I wrote most of this chapter, the House Judiciary Committee approved the Marijuana Opportunity Reinvestment and Expungement (MORE) Act of 2019.

Then, on December 4, 2020, the House made history by becoming the first chamber of Congress to approve legislation to end federal cannabis prohibition. The Senate didn't follow suit, never even taking up the act for a vote. The bill was passed again by the House on April 1, 2022.[1] As of this writing, the Senate is still dragging its feet. But we inch closer every day—several cannabis-related bills have been introduced or reintroduced since then. And in 2022, President Joe Biden issued a mass pardon for federal convictions for minor possession.

If passed, The MORE Act would remove cannabis from the list of controlled substances, decriminalizing it on a federal level. It would attempt to right some of the

---

1   https://www.sierranevadaally.org/2021/08/26/federal-cannabis
-legislation-at-a-crossroads/.

many wrongs the war on drugs left in its wake—wrongs that my friend and I were privileged enough to avoid so many years ago.

Does the bill do enough? Of course not. We can never truly right the injustices done to so many for so long. But it represents hope.

Still, it may be a long time before we can fully erase the stigma that war has cast on cannabis-based medicine. And that makes me furious: How many people have suffered needlessly because they're afraid of, or biased against, cannabis? How many have accepted the lies of Anslinger, Nixon, Regan, et al., as gospel and flatly rejected a remedy that could have, at the very least, drastically eased symptoms? How many years of research have we lost; how many cures and treatments have we missed out on; how many loved ones have suffered needlessly?

I'm confident I will see both medical and recreational cannabis federally legalized within my lifetime. After nearly a century of political wool-pulling, calculated racism, and carefully managed misinformation, society is finally waking up to the fact that pot is not "the devil weed."

We're seeing through the smoke and mirrors of high-level misdirection; realizing that we've wasted eight decades, trillions of dollars, and countless lives on a pack of lies. Society is starting to understand that cannabis holds the key to a sea change for healthcare, medicine, and the pharmaceutical industry as a whole.

And it's about damn time. Way past it, in fact. It feels like we're gradually waking from a long national nightmare and finally seeing the light for the first time in decades.

The challenge now will be not just staying awake, but ensuring that others open their eyes and see the light as well.

The future of medicine depends on it.

Acknowledgments

I am filled with immense gratitude as I extend my special thanks to my cherished family, dear friends, invaluable mentors, and my dedicated colleagues. Without your unwavering support, guidance, and boundless patience throughout the countless drafts and revisions, this project would have remained a dream. Similar to the intricate process of building a business from the ground up, the journey of writing and publishing a book demands teamwork, expertise, and unwavering commitment. I am profoundly indebted to the multitude of individuals who played a significant role in bringing this project to its completion.

To Patrick O'Donnell, my esteemed editor and coauthor, I express my deepest gratitude. He skillfully transformed my thoughts and personal recollections into a harmonious narrative, offering indispensable advice on what to include (or leave out); and dug into research on the failed war on drugs with unflinching tenacity and persistence.

Thanks also are due to Michael Campbell and his team at Skyhorse for their advice and guidance as we moved this project from dream to fruition.

Lastly, I extend my heartfelt appreciation to you, the reader, for embracing the curious spirit and the courage to embark on this journey. It is my fervent hope that the knowledge you acquire from this book will ignite a flame of inspiration within you, urging you to conduct your own research, question the existing norms, and continue exploring the astounding potential of this unique plant and pharmacology. For far too long, cannabis has been unjustly stigmatized as a scourge, when in truth, it harbors the essential elements to unlock revolutionary cures and treatments, promising a profound shift in the way the world embraces modern medicine.

About the Authors

Dr. Oludare "'Dare" Odumosu is a visionary leader and expert in the corporate pharmaceutical and biotech industry, with more than a decade of experience driving innovation and a track record of global commercial success. Dr. Odumosu holds a PhD in biochemistry, a master's degree in public health-epidemiology and biostatistics, and a bachelor's degree in biology. He is a recognized World Bank Institute–certified public health professional and the author of numerous peer-reviewed scientific papers. As the CEO of Zelira Therapeutics, a publicly listed global biopharmaceutical company, Dr. Odumosu is leading the mission to revolutionize healthcare through the development and commercialization of clinically validated cannabis medicines. Under Dr. Odumosu's guidance, Zelira Therapeutics is at the forefront of validating cannabinoids as approved frontline therapies for a wide range of conditions for which traditional pharmaceuticals have fallen short.

Patrick O'Donnell is an author, ghostwriter, and editor with more than thirty years of real-world journalism and marketing experience in the newspaper, magazine, and digital media industries. An avid environmentalist and advocate for equity, justice, and equal rights for all of humanity, Patrick lives with his two sons in Pennsylvania's Berks County region. He'd much rather be outside than sitting behind a keyboard, and enjoys photography, hiking, kayaking, gardening, and reading.